ALSO BY MARY BERGIN AND JUDY GETHERS

SPAGO DESSERTS

SPAGO CHOCOLATE

SPAGO CHOCOLATE

MARY BERGIN AND JUDY GETHERS

PHOTOGRAPHS BY
ALAN RICHARDSON

RANDOM HOUSE NEW YORK

Random House and colophon are registered trademarks
of Random House, Inc.

Library of Congress Cataloging-in-Publication Data

Bergin, Mary.
Spago chocolate / by Mary Bergin and Judy Gethers.
p.   cm.
Includes index.
ISBN 0-679-44833-0
1. Cookery (Chocolate)   2. Desserts.   3. Spago (Restaurant)
I.   Gethers, Judy.   II. Title.
TX767.C5B46   1999
641.8'6—dc21   98-27258

Random House website address: www.atrandom.com

PRINTED IN THE UNITED STATES OF AMERICA ON ACID-FREE PAPER
2 4 6 8 9 7 5 3
FIRST EDITION

Book design by Barbara M. Bachman

CONTENTS

INTRODUCTION

. . .

*O*ne of life's great pleasures is the taste of chocolate. Writing about chocolate evokes many wonderful memories of my childhood. I can still recall the sheer ecstasy of the first bite of an ice cream concoction, or a chewy cookie, or a frosted cake.

My sister Cathy, who is seven years older than me, was my inspiration in the kitchen. One day, out of the blue, she decided to make an angel food cake from scratch. I was amazed; the only cakes I had tasted had come from a box. One bite and I was hooked. This, I thought, is what I want to do. When Cathy opened up a trendy restaurant in West Hollywood and asked me to join her, I jumped at the chance. We had a part-time pastry cook then, and when she quit one day I became the de facto dessert chef.

I have Rudi Gernreich, the designer of the topless bathing suit, to thank for nudging me to Spago. He was a big supporter of mine and a constant inspiration. Rudi came into the kitchen one night and showed me how to make a Sachertorte. It was my first professional dessert. Rudi told me about a friend of his named Puck who was opening a restaurant. He kept pushing me to go for an interview. At his urging, every day after work for four days in a row I walked (I didn't have a car then) to Spago, which was under construction at the time, and every day there was no one to talk to. Finally, on the fifth day, I went upstairs and saw a desk and chair and said to myself, I'm sitting here until someone comes whom I can talk to. Sure enough, after an hour or so a man appeared and asked me who I was and what I wanted. I was so angry by then that I shouted at this unsuspecting person, "Do I have a job here or what?" The man was Wolfgang Puck. I guess he liked my spunk, because he hired me on the spot.

Some of my fondest memories involve Spago's famous Academy Award parties. Back in 1986, while I was looking through the aisles of Gloria's Cake and Candy Supplies store in California, I noticed a candy mold in the shape of an Oscar. On a whim, I decided to buy it.

While we were preparing for our annual Oscar gala that year, Wolfgang told me that Irving "Swifty" Lazar, the host of this big bash, was celebrating his birthday on the night of the party and Wolfgang wanted to make a special cake for him. I realized I had the perfect centerpiece. I made a milk chocolate Oscar, decorated it with gold leaf, and stood it up in the center of his cake. Swifty loved it!

In 1989, my Oscar got his big break: Wolfgang wanted chocolate Oscars for all the tables. We made about three hundred of them. The night of the party, Wolfgang and I were standing in the pastry kitchen with cameras flashing all around us. He held up one of the Oscars, gave a little of its background, and then proceeded to bite its head off. Wolfgang—and my headless Oscar—got a standing ovation.

I hope the chocolate desserts in this book will help you create your own wonderful memories—and maybe even earn you a standing ovation!

Mary Bergin

. . .

I've known Wolfgang Puck since he was twenty-four years old, soon after he arrived in this country, when English was still difficult for him. He was a quick study and had an entertaining wit, and in a short while he could banter with the liveliest. And I've known Mary since she was twenty-six, when she first started at Spago. She had two young children but still succeeded in putting in a full day in the pastry kitchen. Working with them has been a wonderful experience that allowed me to cook and bake and learn. For someone who loves nothing more, it was a match made in heaven. I cannot think of anything else I would rather be doing.

When Mary moved to Las Vegas to open the Spago there, I thought it would be difficult for us to continue as a team, but the kitchen staff was very cooperative and understanding. They let me work at all hours.

So, for the privilege of doing what I love best, I have to thank not only Wolfgang and Mary, but the entire kitchen staff in Las Vegas and Los Angeles.

Judy Fjullros

ALL ABOUT CHOCOLATE

. . .

*T*he Greeks called it: *theobroma cacao,* or "food of the gods." And who are we to question that?

The history of chocolate dates back to the early New World explorers who talked about a bitter drink enjoyed by the natives. Many thought that this bitter chocolate drink contained aphrodisiac qualities, and to this day, chocolate continues to be associated with love. Probably more chocolates are sold on Valentine's Day than at any other time of the year.

The cocoa tree, first discovered in South America, found its way to Mexico around the sixth century, and the cocoa bean was cultivated by the Aztecs and Mayans. When the Spanish decided to add sugar and spices to this bitter drink, the result was much more palatable, particularly pleasing to European taste.

The Spanish tried to keep this discovery to themselves, but chocolate turned up in France, Italy, and England. The city of London boasted many chocolate houses, which became as popular as some of London's most exclusive clubs.

Today, Africa is the largest grower of cocoa beans, and Central America is the smallest. And cocoa is now grown in Hawaii, a new development. There is a considerable difference of opinion among doctors as to the effects of chocolate on the human body. But what they do agree on is that chocolate stimulates the release of endorphins, which resemble opiates and can raise our pain threshhold.

Cocoa beans are taken from large pods growing on the trunks and branches of cacao trees. The pods are round, smooth, and not very elongated. They usually ripen in five to six months and are then harvested. The pods are cut open and the beans, whitish in color, are transferred to large baskets where the seven-to-ten-day fermentation process begins. After fermentation, the beans are spread out on platforms to dry, a process that takes at least five days, and as they dry, the color deepens. The beans are then graded, bagged, and shipped out for roasting. To enhance their flavor, they are roasted at a very low temperature. The beans are then broken open and the inside seeds, called nibs, are ground to a thick liquid that is known as *chocolate liquor.* This liquid also contains a certain amount of fat, called *cocoa butter,* which is pressed out of the liquor by a process invented by a Dutchman, Van Houten.

The next stage is refining. The chocolate is broken up into coarse pieces and ground. *Unsweetened* or *bitter* chocolate is almost pure cocoa liquor, with very little cocoa butter, and is usually sold in packages containing 1-ounce squares. *Semisweet* or *bittersweet* chocolate is the liquor improved with sugar and additional cocoa butter. *Sweet* chocolate has even more of a sugar content and far less cocoa butter and cocoa liquor. It is seldom used for baking. *Milk* chocolate contains milk solids, as well as sugar, cocoa butter, and cocoa liquor. *White* chocolate really isn't chocolate at all. It does not contain cocoa solids but is a combination of cocoa butter, milk solids, and sugar. *Couverture* has a large amount of cocoa butter and is better for glazing and/or dipping. It is not readily available, usually sold in bulk.

To make cocoa powder, most of the cocoa butter is removed from the chocolate, the resulting mass is ground to a powder, and sugar is added.

All chocolate should be stored in a dark, dry area. Dark chocolate should keep at least one year, milk chocolate about six months.

SPAGO CHOCOLATE

CAKES

BUTTERMILK LAYER CAKE 5

SIX-LAYER CASSATA 7

CHOCOLATE ANGEL FOOD CAKE 10

CHOCOLATE CHIFFON CAKE 13

FUDGY CHOCOLATE CAKE 15

GRAND MARNIER CHOCOLATE CAKE 18

INDIVIDUAL CHOCOLATE-HAZELNUT CAKES 21

SPECIAL-OCCASION MASCARPONE LAYER CAKE 23

MARY'S OLD-FASHIONED CHOCOLATE REFRIGERATOR CAKE 27

CLASSIC CHOCOLATE TRUFFLE CAKE 29

ROULADE AU CHOCOLAT POUR JULIA 32

HAZELNUT CHIFFON CAKE 37

MARBLED POUND CAKE 39

CHOCOLATE CRAQUELINE MOUSSE CAKE 43

*S*pago customers love our chocolate cakes. Not a day goes by without someone telling us about his or her favorite. These chocolate lovers share one thing in common: They all wish that they could duplicate our desserts at home.

Now they can.

Besides baking the desserts on the menu, Mary is inundated with special requests. Usually it is for some form of chocolate cake. In this chapter, we have tried to include many of the all-time favorites. Whether on the menu or by special request, they are all extraordinary.

Before you start, remember a few basic rules. Follow these and you will be assured of quality results. First and foremost, always read through the recipe carefully. Second, make certain that you have the proper equipment. Third, follow the directions. Forget about a "pinch" of this or a "handful" of that. Exact measurements are crucial to the outcome whether it pertains to cake layers, the filling, or the frosting. In other words, cake making is a science, not an improvisation.

There is one last bit of advice we'd like to offer: Enjoy yourself. Baking should be fun from the moment you decide on a recipe to the moment of truth, eating what you have made.

. . .

BUTTERMILK LAYER CAKE

Makes one 9-inch round cake
Serves 8 to 10

Cut into layers and frosted with our Chocolate Frosting, this becomes a very festive cake, perfect for special occasions. At Spago, we decorate each slice with milk chocolate curls and place on a pool of chocolate sauce or crème anglaise flavored with Bailey's or Godiva liqueur. It is one of the more popular birthday cakes. But because it is so easy to make, it could become your everyday cake.

EQUIPMENT: 9-inch round cake pan, sifter, electric mixer with large bowl, 9-inch cardboard round, long serrated knife

1¾ CUPS ALL-PURPOSE FLOUR

2 TEASPOONS BAKING POWDER

½ TEASPOON BAKING SODA

½ TEASPOON SALT

¾ CUP GRANULATED SUGAR *I used salted*

4 OUNCES (1 STICK) UNSALTED BUTTER,
    AT ROOM TEMPERATURE, CUT INTO
    SMALL PIECES

4 EGG YOLKS

1 CUP BUTTERMILK

DOUBLE RECIPE CHOCOLATE FROSTING
    (SEE PAGE 208)

I doubled the cake recipe but still did not need to double the frosting recipe

2/3's down - it browned too quickly on top.

1. Position the rack in the center of the oven and preheat the oven to 350 degrees. Butter or coat with vegetable spray a 9-inch round cake pan. Dust with flour, tapping out any excess flour. Set aside.

2. Sift together the flour, baking powder, baking soda, and salt. Set aside.

3. In the large bowl of an electric mixer fitted with a paddle or beaters, beat the sugar and butter. Start on low speed until slightly blended, then gradually turn to high and beat until fluffy. Add the yolks, one at a time, beating just to combine after each addition. Turn the speed to low, and alternate adding the flour mixture and buttermilk, starting and ending with the flour mixture (three additions of flour and two of buttermilk).

4. Scrape the batter into the prepared pan and gently tap the pan on the work surface to level. Bake until a cake tester gently inserted into the center of the cake comes out

clean, about 45 minutes. Cool on a rack for 15 minutes, then invert onto a cardboard round and place back on the rack to cool completely.

5. Using a long serrated knife, cut the cake into two equal round halves (see page 227). Then cut each half into halves, giving you four equal rounds. Brush off excess crumbs before frosting. (If you really feel expert enough, each of the four layers can be cut in half, giving you eight thin layers. However, this is not for the fainthearted or the beginner.)

6. Save the best layer for the top. Divide the frosting equally, depending on how many layers you have, into either four or eight parts. Place the first layer on the cardboard round and spread the top of the layer with frosting. Repeat with the remaining layers and finish by frosting the sides.

7. To serve, set the finished cake on a large round serving plate. Garnish with mint leaves and fresh strawberries or milk chocolate curls.

TO PREPARE AHEAD: Through step 4, the cake can be prepared 1 day ahead. Through step 6, the cake should be finished early in the day it is being served and refrigerated. Remove the cake from the refrigerator about 30 minutes before serving.

SIX-LAYER CASSATA

Makes one 8½-inch loaf
Serves 8 to 10

Cassata, a Sicilian dessert served at Easter, is an Italian sponge cake layered with a rich ricotta filling. The cake is baked in two loaf pans, each loaf cut into three layers. We have susbstituted dried cherries for the candied fruit usually found in the filling, and added shaved chocolate. The result is a creamy and delicate treat. For added decadence, we sometimes serve this with vanilla ice cream.

EQUIPMENT: Two 8½ × 4½ × 2½-inch loaf pans, medium heatproof bowl, large whisk, electric mixer with large bowl, long serrated knife, cardboard, pastry brush, small metal spatula, piping bag

8 EGGS	2 TEASPOONS VANILLA EXTRACT
1 CUP GRANULATED SUGAR	⅓ CUP FRANGELICO
1⅓ CUPS ALL-PURPOSE FLOUR	RICOTTA FILLING (SEE PAGE 202)
7 OUNCES (1¾ STICKS) UNSALTED BUTTER, MELTED	CHOCOLATE GLAZE (SEE PAGE 210)

1. Position the rack in the center of the oven and preheat the oven to 350 degrees. Butter or coat with vegetable spray two loaf pans. Dust with flour, tapping out any excess flour.

2. In a medium heatproof bowl set over a pan of simmering water, whisk the eggs. Gradually whisk in the sugar and continue to whisk until the eggs are foamy and thicken slightly.

3. Transfer to the large bowl of an electric mixer fitted with a paddle or beaters. Beat on high speed until thick and pale yellow, 7 to 10 minutes. (This is *very* important for the proper volume.)

4. Remove the bowl from the mixer and fold in the flour, then the melted butter and vanilla. Divide the batter and scrape into the prepared pans, gently tapping the pans on the work surface to level.

5. Bake until golden brown, 25 to 30 minutes, reversing the pans back to front after 15 minutes. A cake tester inserted into the center of one of the cakes should come out clean.

6. Cool on a rack for 15 minutes. Run the point of a sharp knife around the inside of each pan and turn the cakes out on a foil-lined rack. Let cool completely.

7. Cut out a piece of cardboard that will fit into one of the loaf pans. Then cut a piece of parchment paper into a 7 × 14-inch strip. Position the cardboard on the parchment paper so that the long ends of the parchment extend out to the side. (This will make it easier to fit the cake back into the pan as well as lift the cake out of the pan.) Set aside.

8. To assemble, using a long serrated knife, level the tops of the cakes. Cut each cake horizontally into three even layers (see page 227). Save the best of the six layers for the top. Set the first layer on the cardboard and brush lightly with Frangelico. Then, using a small metal spatula, spread $1/4$ cup plus 2 tablespoons of the Ricotta Filling evenly over the layer. Carefully place the next layer on top and repeat with the Frangelico and the Ricotta Filling. Continue with the remaining layers, Frangelico, and Ricotta Filling. You will have six layers of cake and five layers of filling.

9. Carefully lift the ends of the parchment paper and fit the cake into one of the pans, the paper extending over the sides of the pan. Refrigerate for at least 30 minutes.

10. Remove the pan from the refrigerator. Holding both ends of the parchment paper, lift the cake from the pan and place on a rack. Slip the paper out from under the cardboard and fit the rack into a baking tray. Drizzle Chocolate Glaze over the cake and allow to set completely. Refrigerate until needed, 2 to 3 hours.

11. To serve, cut into slices and garnish with fresh berries. Or, if desired, tiny rosettes of melted white chocolate can be piped around the top (see photo) using a piping bag.

TO PREPARE AHEAD: Through step 6 or 10, the cake can be finished early in the day and then refrigerated.

CHOCOLATE ANGEL FOOD CAKE

Makes one 9-inch cake
or eight 4-inch cakes*
Serves 8

In the restaurant, we bake these small cakes in individual tins and serve them with Mocha Zabaione (see page 146), but they can also simply be dusted with sifted confectioners' sugar. They are delicious with or without the sauce, and it's a perfect way to use egg whites that have been frozen.**

EQUIPMENT: sifter, electric mixer with large bowl, large rubber spatula, 9-inch angel food tube pan with removable bottom, 9-inch cardboard round

¾ **CUP CAKE FLOUR**	**1 TEASPOON CREAM OF TARTAR**
1 CUP CONFECTIONERS' SUGAR	½ **TEASPOON SALT**
½ **CUP UNSWEETENED COCOA POWDER**	**1 CUP GRANULATED SUGAR, SIFTED**
1 TABLESPOON INSTANT ESPRESSO	**1 TEASPOON VANILLA EXTRACT**
1½ **CUPS (ABOUT 11 LARGE) EGG WHITES,**	
AT ROOM TEMPERATURE	

1. Position the rack in the center of the oven and preheat the oven to 350 degrees.

2. Sift together the flour, confectioners' sugar, cocoa, and espresso four times. Set aside.

3. In the large bowl of an electric mixer fitted with a whip or beaters, whip the egg whites until frothy. Add the cream of tartar and salt, and continue to beat until soft peaks begin to form. Gradually pour in the granulated sugar and vanilla, and continue to whip until the whites are shiny and firm but not stiff, and have doubled in volume.

---

* To make the smaller cakes, in step 5, scrape the batter into eight 4-inch tube pans, preferably nonstick. Bake until the cake springs back when lightly touched, 20 to 25 minutes. Remove from the oven and invert over a rack. Allow the cakes to slip out by themselves. If they don't, let them cool, then use the knife blade to separate them from the pan. (Smaller cakes pop out of pans more easily than larger cakes.) Cool completely. Remove each cake as described in step 7.

** Egg whites can be frozen in plastic containers. Mark the containers with the number of whites in each. Defrost in the refrigerator and then bring to room temperature.

4. Remove the bowl from the mixer and sprinkle about one-fourth of the sifted ingredients over the top and, using a large rubber spatula, carefully but quickly fold the mixture into the egg whites, turning the bowl as you fold. Repeat this procedure until all the flour mixture is incorporated into the egg whites. Do this as quickly as possible so that the whites retain as much of their volume as possible.

5. Carefully scrape the batter into an *ungreased* 9-inch angel food tube pan. Using the rubber spatula, cut through the batter to eliminate any air bubbles, and then level with the spatula.

6. Bake until the cake springs back when lightly touched, about 55 minutes. Remove from the oven and invert over a narrow-necked bottle that will support the cake. (It's a good idea to test the pan before you fill it to make certain it will fit over the neck of the bottle.) Cool completely.

7. When cool, remove the pan from the bottle and turn it right side up. Loosen the cake from the pan by carefully running a long knife around the sides of the pan and around the center tube, separating the cake from the pan. Push the bottom up, removing the cake from the outer pan. Again, using the knife, loosen the cake from the bottom of the pan and invert onto a cardboard round.

8. To serve, if desired, spoon Mocha Zabaione Sauce on a dessert plate and place a slice of cake on the sauce. Arrange a scoop of whipped cream on the side and decorate the plate with shaved milk chocolate.

TO PREPARE AHEAD: Through step 7, the cake can be made the day before needed.

CHOCOLATE CHIFFON CAKE

Makes two 8- or
9-inch round cakes
Each serves 8

Our chocolate book wouldn't be complete without including the Chocolate Chiffon Cake. This is a light, versatile cake that is the foundation for many cakes we serve at Spago. The cake freezes well, so if you want to use only one of the layers, the second layer can be double wrapped in plastic wrap and frozen for another time.

EQUIPMENT: two 8- or 9-inch round cake pans, sifter, electric mixer with 2 large bowls, rubber spatula, 9-inch cardboard round

1 ½ **CUPS GRANULATED SUGAR**	¾ **CUP VEGETABLE OIL**
1 **CUP ALL-PURPOSE FLOUR**	½ **CUP WATER**
¾ **CUP UNSWEETENED COCOA POWDER**	1 **TEASPOON VANILLA EXTRACT**
2 **TEASPOONS BAKING POWDER**	2 **EGG WHITES**
1 **TEASPOON BAKING SODA**	**FROSTING OF YOUR CHOICE (SEE FILLINGS**
¼ **TEASPOON SALT**	**AND SAUCES CHAPTER)**
4 **EGGS, SEPARATED**	

1. Position the rack in the center of the oven and preheat the oven to 350 degrees. Butter or coat with vegetable spray two 8- or 9-inch round cake pans. Dust with flour, tapping out any excess flour. Set aside.

2. Sift together 1 cup of the sugar, the flour, cocoa, baking powder, baking soda, and salt. Set aside.

3. In the large bowl of an electric mixer fitted with a paddle or beaters, beat the egg yolks at high speed. Turn the speed to low and slowly pour in the oil, water, and vanilla. Gradually add the sifted ingredients and, when almost incorporated, turn the speed to medium, and beat until well combined. Remove the bowl from the mixer.

4. In another clean large bowl, with a whip or clean beaters, whip the 6 egg whites until soft peaks form. Start on medium speed and raise the speed as the peaks begin to form. Gradually pour in the remaining ½ cup sugar and whip until the whites are shiny and firm, but not stiff. With a rubber spatula, fold one-fourth of the whites into

the chocolate mixture, then scrape the chocolate mixture back into the whites, quickly folding until completely incorporated.

5. Scrape into the prepared pans and bake until the edges of the cake pull away from the pan and a tester gently inserted into the middle of the cake comes out clean, about 30 minutes. Cool on a rack. To remove, run a sharp knife around the inside of each pan to loosen the cake. Invert onto a rack to cool completely. Place a 9-inch cardboard round on the cake and invert the cake onto it.

6. There are many ways to serve this cake. You can dust the rounds with sifted confectioners' sugar, cut them into slices, and serve them with Drambouie-Flavored Crème Anglaise (page 205) spooned under or over each slice. Or you can build a layer cake using the two layers, or cut each layer in half horizontally and frost them with the frosting of your choice.

TO PREPARE AHEAD: Through step 5, the cake can be made 1 day ahead.

FUDGY CHOCOLATE CAKE

Makes one 10-inch cake
Serves 8 to 10

This wonderfully moist, fudgy cake can be made in a 10-inch bundt pan, as below, or in two 9 × 5 × 3-inch loaf pans (baking time will be 35 to 40 minutes). We first tasted this cake when Jean-Paul DeSourdie, a caterer in New York, brought it as a gift. We liked it so much we decided that, with our minor additions, it belonged in the Spago repertoire.

EQUIPMENT: 10-inch bundt pan, sifter, medium heatproof bowl, electric mixer with large bowl, 10-inch cardboard round

2 CUPS ALL-PURPOSE FLOUR	2 CUPS GRANULATED SUGAR
1 TEASPOON BAKING SODA	1 TABLESPOON VANILLA EXTRACT
½ TEASPOON SALT	2 CUPS COLD BREWED COFFEE
12 OUNCES BITTERSWEET CHOCOLATE,	3 TABLESPOONS GRAND MARNIER OR
CUT INTO SMALL PIECES	KAHLÚA
8 OUNCES (2 STICKS) UNSALTED BUTTER,	GRAND MARNIER SAUCE, OPTIONAL
CUT INTO SMALL PIECES	(SEE PAGE 204)
2 EGGS	

1. Position the rack in the center of the oven and preheat the oven to 325 degrees. Butter or coat with vegetable spray a 10-inch bundt pan, making certain you coat all the ridges plus the center tube. If the pan does not have a nonstick coating, dust it with flour, tapping out any excess flour. Set aside.

2. Sift together the flour, baking soda, and salt. Set aside.

3. In a medium heatproof bowl set over a pan of gently simmering water, melt the chocolate and butter, stirring occasionally. When almost melted, turn off the heat, and let melt completely.

4. In the large bowl of an electric mixer fitted with a paddle or beaters, whip the eggs. On low speed, gradually pour in the sugar and continue to beat until well incorporated, raising the speed when all the sugar has been incorporated. On low speed, scrape in the melted chocolate mixture, add the vanilla, and mix well.

5. Alternate adding the flour mixture and the coffee, starting and ending with the flour mixture (three additions of flour and two of coffee). Do the additions on low speed and then turn the speed to high. Stop the machine occasionally and scrape around the bowl and under the beaters. Add the Grand Marnier and beat just until combined.

6. Scrape the batter into the prepared pan, distributing it evenly around the pan (tap the pan to level the batter). Bake until a cake tester inserted in the middle of the cake comes out clean, about 1 hour. Cool on a rack for 15 minutes, then invert onto a 10-inch cardboard round and return to the rack to cool completely.

7. To serve, cut the cake into slices, and serve with a dollop of whipped cream. Scatter a few fresh raspberries or sliced strawberries around the cake. Or spoon a little Grand Marnier Sauce around the center of each plate and set a piece of cake on the sauce.

TO PREPARE AHEAD: Through step 6, the cake can be made 1 day ahead.

GRAND MARNIER CHOCOLATE CAKE

Makes one 9-inch cake

Serves 8 to 10

This is an adaptation of a chocolate bourbon cake that Melinda Lucas created when she was a pastry chef at one of Wolfgang Puck's restaurants. If you prefer a flavor other than Grand Marnier (Tuaca or Amaretto), by all means, use it. We suggest using instant coffee dissolved in boiling water. However, 1½ cups strong coffee or decaffeinated espresso can be substituted. An electric mixer is not needed for this cake—just a large heatproof bowl, a whisk, and a strong arm.

EQUIPMENT: 9-inch round springform pan, sifter, large heatproof bowl, whisk

2 CUPS ALL-PURPOSE FLOUR

1 TEASPOON BAKING SODA

½ TEASPOON SALT

8 OUNCES BITTERSWEET CHOCOLATE, CUT
    INTO SMALL PIECES

4 OUNCES (1 STICK) UNSALTED BUTTER, CUT
    INTO SMALL PIECES

⅓ CUP GRAND MARNIER

3 TABLESPOONS INSTANT ESPRESSO,
    DISSOLVED IN 1½ CUPS BOILING
    WATER

1½ CUPS GRANULATED SUGAR

2 EGGS, LIGHTLY BEATEN

1 TEASPOON VANILLA EXTRACT

1. Place the rack in the center of the oven and preheat the oven to 325 degrees. Butter or coat with vegetable spray a 9-inch round springform pan. Dust with sifted cocoa, tapping out any excess cocoa. Set aside.

2. Sift together the flour, baking soda, and salt. Set aside.

3. In a large heatproof bowl placed over a pan of simmering water, melt the chocolate and butter, stirring occasionally. When they are almost melted, remove from the heat and let melt completely.

4. Whisk in the Grand Marnier and coffee, then the sugar, the eggs, and finally the vanilla. Whisk until completely incorporated. Whisk in the flour mixture until smooth.

5. Pour into the prepared pan and bake until a cake tester inserted in the middle of the cake comes out clean, 60 to 65 minutes. Cool on a rack.

6. To serve, cut the cake into slices and serve with a scoop of David's Orange-You-Glad-It's-Chocolate Ice Cream (see page 178) or the ice cream of your choice. The cake can also be served with a dollop of whipped cream.

TO PREPARE AHEAD: Through step 5, the cake can be made 1 day ahead.

INDIVIDUAL CHOCOLATE-HAZELNUT CAKES

Makes twelve 3-inch cakes

At Spago, we bake these cakes in special tins that we have made specifically for us. The tins are round circles of stainless steel, 3 inches in diameter and 1½ inches high. You can use ramekins of the same dimensions. This is a rich dessert and, accompanied by Drambuie-Flavored Crème Anglaise, a particularly flavorful one.

EQUIPMENT: 12 muffin tins or ramekins, 3 inches in diameter and 1½ inches deep, medium heatproof bowl, whip or egg beater, electric mixer with 2 large bowls, food processor, rubber spatula

12 OUNCES BITTERSWEET CHOCOLATE, CUT INTO SMALL PIECES	DRAMBUIE-FLAVORED CRÈME ANGLAISE (SEE PAGE 205)
1 CUP HEAVY CREAM	WHIPPED CREAM
6 EGGS	11 OUNCES (2¼ CUPS) HAZELNUTS, TOASTED**
½ CUP GRANULATED SUGAR	
HAZELNUT PASTE*	
SIFTED CONFECTIONERS' SUGAR	

1. Position the rack in the center of the oven and preheat the oven to 350 degrees. Butter or coat with vegetable spray 12 muffin tins or ramekins. Dust with flour, tapping out any excess flour. Set aside.

2. In a medium heatproof bowl set over a pan of simmering water, melt the chocolate. When it is almost melted, turn off the heat and allow it to melt completely, stirring occasionally. Chocolate should be warm, not hot, when used.

3. In a large bowl using a whip or eggbeater, whip the cream. You should have 2 cups whipped cream. Refrigerate, covered, until needed.

---

* To make the hazelnut paste, place the remaining hazelnuts plus 2 tablespoons hazelnut oil (or unflavored vegetable oil) in the workbowl of a food processor fitted with a steel blade and process until a paste forms. The paste will stick to the sides and bottom of the bowl.

** To toast the hazelnuts, spread over a baking tray and toast in a preheated 350-degree oven for 10 to 12 minutes, turning the nuts after 5 or 6 minutes. Let cool, place in a clean towel, and rub off as much of the skins as possible. Measure a scant cup of hazelnuts and chop fine to use as garnish. Set aside.

4. In the large bowl of an electric mixer fitted with a paddle or beaters, on high speed beat the eggs and sugar until thick and pale yellow in color, about 8 to 10 minutes. Stop the mixer and scrape the melted chocolate into the egg mixture, then add the hazelnut paste, and beat on high speed until well mixed. Stop the machine occasionally and scrape down the sides of the bowl and under the beaters using a rubber spatula.

5. Remove the bowl from the mixer and stir in about one-third of the whipped cream. Scrape the egg mixture back into the whipped cream and fold through.

6. Fill the tins or ramekins three-quarters full. (If using the same tin or ramekin again, after baking, cool, clean as needed, spray, and flour.) Bake until the top is fairly firm to the touch, but the center is still soft, about 20 minutes. Cool on a rack. To remove the cake, run a sharp knife around the inside of the tin or ramekin, loosening the cake, and unmold the cake onto a flat surface.

7. To serve, place one cake in the center of a plate and sift confectioners' sugar over the top. Spoon Drambuie-Flavored Crème Anglaise around each cake and place a large dollop of whipped cream on top. Garnish with a sprinkling of chopped hazelnuts and place a mint leaf in the cream. Top with a few chocolate curls, if desired. You can also decorate the outside rim of each plate with dots of Raspberry or Strawberry Compote (see page 216), if desired.

TO PREPARE AHEAD: Through step 6, the cakes can be made early in the day. When cool, refrigerate the cakes, removing them about 30 minutes before serving.

SPECIAL-OCCASION MASCARPONE LAYER CAKE

Makes one 8- or
9-inch round cake
Serves 12 to 14

At Spago, we bake the Chocolate Chiffon Cake on a large sheet pan and cut it into 3-inch circles, which we then moisten, layer, and frost for individual servings. However, the recipe below is far more practical and much easier to assemble at home. This is definitely a cake to reserve for a special occasion.

EQUIPMENT: small bowl, electric mixer with large bowl, small saucepan, whisk, long serrated knife, soft pastry brush, 9-inch cardboard round, small offset spatula, wire rack set into baking pan

CHOCOLATE CHIFFON CAKE (SEE PAGE 13)

COFFEE SOAKING LIQUID
1/2 CUP BREWED ESPRESSO OR STRONG
    COFFEE, WARMED SLIGHTLY
1/2 CUP WATER
1/4 CUP GRANULATED SUGAR
2 TABLESPOONS RUM
2 TABLESPOONS KAHLÚA

MASCARPONE FILLING
6 EGGS
1/4 CUP GRANULATED SUGAR
1 POUND MASCARPONE CHEESE
3 TABLESPOONS RUM
3 TABLESPOONS KAHLÚA
4 OUNCES MILK CHOCOLATE, GRATED
2 GELATIN SHEETS* OR 1 ENVELOPE
    UNFLAVORED GELATIN POWDER
GANACHE (SEE PAGE 209), WARMED

1. Make the Chocolate Chiffon Cake as directed. Set aside until needed.

2. Make the coffee soaking liquid: In a small bowl, combine the coffee, water, and sugar, stirring until the sugar dissolves completely. Add the 2 tablespoons each of rum and Kahlúa. Set aside until needed.

3. Make the mascarpone filling: In the large bowl of an electric mixer fitted with a paddle or beaters, beat the eggs with the sugar on high speed until very thick, pale yellow, and doubled in volume, about 8 to 10 minutes. Turn down the speed, add the

* Gelatin sheets are used in most restaurants. They can be found in gourmet shops and food catalogs. The sheets melt more easily and have less flavor than the powder.

mascarpone cheese and 2 tablespoons each of rum and Kahlúa, and beat until well combined, stopping the machine and scraping down the sides of the bowl and under the beaters as necessary. Remove the bowl from the mixer and fold in the grated chocolate.

4. In a small saucepan, heat the remaining 1 tablespoon each of rum and Kahlúa and dissolve the gelatin. Whisk into the mascarpone mixture and place the bowl into a larger bowl filled with ice cubes and cold water until thick enough to spread. (Or this can be refrigerated until thickened.)

5. Prepare the cake for filling and frosting: On a flat work surface, using a long serrated knife (see page 227), cut each cake layer in half horizontally. With a soft pastry brush, brush away any excess cake crumbs.

6. Reserving the best layer for the top, place the first cake layer on a 9-inch cardboard round. Using a pastry brush, moisten, but do not saturate, the layer with the soaking liquid. With a small offset spatula, spread a scant 2 cups of the mascarpone filling over the layer. Set the second layer on the filling, pressing down gently to secure, and repeat with the soaking liquid and scant 2 cups of filling. Repeat again with the third layer and remaining filling. Top with the last layer and lightly moisten with the coffee soaking liquid. Wrap the cake in plastic wrap and refrigerate overnight.

7. The next day, remove the cake from the refrigerator, carefully unwrap, and place on a wire rack set into a baking pan. Pour the warm Ganache over the cake, covering it entirely, and return to the refrigerator, pan and all, until the Ganache sets, 20 to 30 minutes. Remove from the refrigerator and transfer the cake to a plate. Scrape the Ganache that has fallen into the baking pan into a small saucepan.

8. To serve, set a slice of cake on a plate. Reheat the Ganache and decorate each plate with tiny pools of the Ganache.

TO PREPARE AHEAD: Through step 6. Through step 7, the cake should be finished early in the day being served.

MARY'S OLD-FASHIONED CHOCOLATE
REFRIGERATOR CAKE

Serves 10

When Mary was a child, this was a favorite cake in her household, using store-bought chocolate wafers. Our version is so much more delicious, made with homemade cookies. When we were testing the recipe in the Spago kitchen, Zinna, one of Mary's assistants, suggested that we decorate the cake like an old-fashioned refrigerator. It was a stroke of genius!

You can whip the cream as the cookies are baking, and refrigerate it, covered, until needed. Whisk a few times before spreading on the cookies.

EQUIPMENT: 1 or 2 baking trays, rolling pin, 2¾-inch cookie cutter, large flat tray, piping bag, small heatproof bowl, long serrated knife

CHOCOLATE PÂTE SUCRÉE (SEE PAGE 72)
3 CUPS HEAVY CREAM, WHIPPED

2 OUNCES BITTERSWEET CHOCOLATE,
CUT INTO SMALL PIECES

1. Line one or two baking trays with parchment paper.

2. Make the cookies: Follow the recipe for Chocolate Pâte Sucrée. On a lightly floured surface, roll the dough out to a rectangle, about 12 × 20 inches. Using a 2¾-inch cookie cutter, cut out 24 circles. Gently press the scraps of dough together and roll out to a rectangle about 12 × 10 inches. Cut out the remaining 12 circles. As the cookies are cut out, arrange them on the prepared baking trays. Refrigerate until firm, about 30 minutes.

3. Set the rack in the middle of the oven and preheat the oven to 350 degrees.

4. Remove the baking trays from the refrigerator. Prick the cookies with the tines of a fork, making a decorative pattern. Bake until crisp, 13 to 14 minutes, reversing the trays back to front after 7 minutes. Cool on a rack.

5. Make the cake: Spread a thick layer of whipped cream on one side of a cookie and gently press a second cookie against the whipped cream. Spread cream on the unfrosted side of the second cookie and press the third cookie against the second. Continue layering with cream and cookies until you have a *long row* of nine cookies. Carefully lay the row of cookies on a large flat tray. Make another set of nine cookies and whipped cream and lay it right next to the first row. Make a third and fourth row, placing each alongside the first two rows (see photos below). Spread the remaining whipped cream over and around the cookies, covering the entire surface, leveling with a small spatula. Refrigerate until needed.

6. In a small heatproof bowl set over a pan of simmering water, melt the chocolate until almost melted. Remove from the heat and let melt completely, stirring once or twice. Prepare a small piping bag made with parchment paper (see page 223). Spoon the melted chocolate into the piping bag, cut a tiny opening at the very tip, and decorate the top of cake as you wish (perhaps to resemble the outside of a refrigerator-freezer). Return the cake to the refrigerator until serving time.

7. To serve, slip a wide metal spatula under the cake and set it on a flat serving plate. Surround with fresh berries. (This is something you want all your guests to see.) Using a long serrated knife, cut the cake across the four rows into thin slices. Place a slice on a dessert plate and garnish with a few of the berries.

TO PREPARE AHEAD: Cookies can be made 1 day ahead. Through step 5, the cake should be finished early in the day.

STEP 5: MAKING THE CAKE

CLASSIC CHOCOLATE TRUFFLE CAKE

Makes eight 4-inch cakes
Serves 8

Mary has made this Spago classic on TV many times, and it is one of the most frequently requested recipes in the restaurant. If you want to save time or don't want to make your own truffles, a good-quality chocolate truffle from a reputable chocolate shop will work almost as well. When raspberries are not at their best, eliminate them from the truffles and pipe plain chocolate mounds instead.

EQUIPMENT: 2 small heatproof bowls, baking tray, pastry bag with #3 plain tip, 8 oversize muffin cups or 1¼-cup custard cups, electric mixer with large bowl, rubber spatula

TRUFFLES	CHOCOLATE CAKE
4 OUNCES BITTERSWEET OR SEMISWEET CHOCOLATE, CUT INTO SMALL PIECES	5 OUNCES BITTERSWEET CHOCOLATE, CUT INTO SMALL PIECES
3 TABLESPOONS HEAVY CREAM	5 OUNCES (1¼ STICKS) UNSALTED BUTTER, CUT INTO SMALL PIECES
½ OUNCE (1 TABLESPOON) UNSALTED BUTTER	3 EGGS, AT ROOM TEMPERATURE
2 TABLESPOONS FLAVORING OF CHOICE (GRAND MARNIER, FRAMBOISE, CHAMBORD, OR VANILLA EXTRACT)	3 EGG YOLKS, AT ROOM TEMPERATURE
8 FRESH PERFECT RASPBERRIES, OPTIONAL	½ CUP GRANULATED SUGAR
	5 TABLESPOONS PLUS 1 TEASPOON ALL-PURPOSE FLOUR

1. Make the truffles: In a small heatproof bowl set over a pan of simmering water, combine the chocolate, cream, and butter. When almost melted, remove from the heat and stir the mixture until smooth. Stir in the flavoring of your choice and refrigerate until thick enough to mound on a spoon, stirring occasionally, about 30 minutes. Do not let it get too hard since you want to pipe it.

2. Line a baking tray with parchment or wax paper. Scrape the chocolate mixture into a pastry bag fitted with a #3 plain tip. Pipe eight 1-inch mounds onto the prepared tray. Place one raspberry in the center of each chocolate mound and pipe a little more of the chocolate mixture on top to enclose completely. It will resemble a chocolate beehive. Refrigerate until firm, about 15 minutes.

3. Make the cakes: Position the rack in the center of the oven and preheat the oven to 350 degrees. Butter or coat with vegetable spray 8 oversize muffin cups (4 inches wide and 2 inches deep) or 1¼-cup custard cups. Line the bottoms with rounds of wax paper. (To cut out the rounds, place one of the cups on wax paper and trace around the bottom with a pencil. Then cut out the eight circles, and place them pencil-side down in the cups.) Set aside.

4. In a small heatproof bowl set over a pan of simmering water, melt together the chocolate and butter. This should be very liquid. Cool slightly.

5. Meanwhile, in the large bowl of an electric mixer fitted with paddle or beaters, on high speed, beat the eggs, egg yolks, and sugar until tripled in volume, about 5 minutes. Scrape in the chocolate mixture and, on low speed, beat just until combined. Remove the bowl from the mixer and fold in the flour, using a rubber spatula. Spoon a little of the batter into each of the prepared cups and set one truffle on top, but do not push it down; cover with the remaining batter. Arrange the cups on a baking tray and bake until the edges of the cakes begin to pull away from the sides of the cups, 12 to 13 minutes. Let stand 10 minutes, then invert onto individual dessert plates and carefully peel off the papers.

6. Serve warm. Dust with sifted confectioners' sugar and spoon softly whipped cream or ice cream next to each cake. If desired, garnish with a few fresh raspberries or Chocolate Curls (see page 213). Serve immediately.

TO PREPARE AHEAD: In step 5, arrange the filled cups on the baking tray and refrigerate until serving time. This can be done 1 day ahead. About 30 minutes before baking, preheat the oven, remove the baking tray from the refrigerator, and continue with the recipe.

ROULADE AU CHOCOLAT POUR JULIA

Makes one 17-inch cake roll

Serves 10 to 12

Mary made a version of this cake for *Baking with Julia,* the television series with Julia Child. (The recipe was included in the cookbook based on the series.) It's based on our Chocolate Chiffon Cake (see page 13), which we spread with filling and then roll, making this the most delectable "jelly" roll you have ever tasted. When the Spago staff sampled the cake, they all came back for second helpings—and they're a tough audience.

EQUIPMENT: 12 × 17 × 2-inch baking tray, sifter, electric mixer with 2 large bowls, rubber spatula, offset spatula, long serrated knife, pastry bag with #3 star tip

1½ **CUPS PLUS 2 TABLESPOONS**	4 **EGGS, SEPARATED**
GRANULATED SUGAR	¾ **CUP VEGETABLE OIL**
1 **CUP ALL-PURPOSE FLOUR**	½ **CUP WATER**
¾ **CUP UNSWEETENED COCOA POWDER**	1 **TEASPOON VANILLA EXTRACT**
2 **TEASPOONS BAKING POWDER**	2 **EGG WHITES**
1 **TEASPOON BAKING SODA**	**CHOCOLATE-HAZELNUT MOUSSE**
¼ **TEASPOON SALT**	**(SEE PAGE 197)**

1. Position the rack in the center of the oven and preheat the oven to 350 degrees. Butter or coat with vegetable spray a baking tray, 12 × 17 × 2 inches. Line with parchment paper and then spray the paper. Set aside.

2. Sift together 1 cup of the sugar, the flour, cocoa, baking powder, baking soda, and salt. Set aside.

3. In the large bowl of an electric mixer fitted with a paddle or beaters, beat the egg yolks at high speed. Turn the machine to low and pour in the oil, water, and vanilla. Gradually add the sifted ingredients and, when almost incorporated, turn the speed to medium and beat until well combined.

4. In another clean large bowl, with whip or clean beaters, whip the 6 egg whites until soft peaks form. Start on medium speed and raise the speed as the peaks begin to form. Gradually pour in the remaining ½ cup sugar and continue to whip until the whites are shiny and firm, but not stiff. With a rubber spatula, fold one-quarter of

the whites into the chocolate mixture, then scrape the chocolate mixture back into the whites, quickly folding until completely incorporated.

5. Scrape into the prepared pan and spread with an offset spatula, smoothing and leveling the top. Bake until the edges of the cake pull away from the pan and the cake springs back when lightly pressed, 25 to 30 minutes. Cool on a rack.

6. When completely cool, place the pan on a firm surface. With a sharp knife, cut around the outside edges of the entire cake, separating the cake from the pan. Sprinkle 2 tablespoons of granulated sugar over the surface of the cake (to prevent sticking when you invert the cake). Invert a second baking tray on the top of the cake and flip the cake over onto the second tray. Carefully peel off the parchment paper, turn the paper over, and place back on the cake. Invert the cake and the paper so that the paper is on the baking tray and the sugared side is on top. You are now ready to spread the filling onto the cake.

7. Fill and roll the cake: Place the cake with one of the 17-inch sides directly in front of you. Using your spatula, spread 1½ cups of the Chocolate-Hazelnut Mousse over the surface of the cake to the edge of three of the sides, leaving about a 1-inch space along the one side directly in front of you (see photo). Level the filling. Refrigerate the remaining mousse, covered.

8. Starting with the 17-inch side in front of you, using the parchment paper to help you, roll the cake toward the opposite side, completely enclosing the filling (see photo). Make certain that you do not roll the paper *into* the cake. Tuck the paper around the rolled cake to secure (see photo). Leave the cake on the pan and refrigerate until the filling is firm, at least 2 hours, up to overnight.

9. To serve, remove the cake from the refrigerator and unroll out of the paper onto a firm surface. Using a long serrated knife, cut a 2-inch diagonal piece off each end. With a #3 star tip fitted into a pastry bag, pipe 10 or 12 rosettes of mousse spaced evenly across the tip of the cake. Dust with sifted confectioners' sugar. Carefully transfer to a serving platter and refrigerate until needed. When ready to serve, cut into 10 or 12 portions. Pass the remaining mousse.

TO PREPARE AHEAD: Through step 8, the cake can be made 1 day ahead. Decorate about 1 hour before serving.

STEP 7: SPREADING THE MOUSSE

STEP 8: ROLLING THE CAKE

STEP 8: USING THE PAPER TO HELP ROLL THE CAKE

STEP 8: TUCKING THE PAPER AROUND THE CAKE

HAZELNUT CHIFFON CAKE

Makes one 10-inch cake
Serves 12 to 14

This recipe, cut in half, is the base for the Hazelnut Domes (see page 63). However, it makes a marvelous layer cake, layered with Ganache, as described below, or Chocolate-Hazelnut Mousse (see page 197) and glazed with Chocolate Glaze. If you don't have a 10 × 3-inch round baking pan, this can be baked in a 10-inch springform pan.

EQUIPMENT: 10 × 3-inch round baking pan, sifter, electric mixer with 2 large bowls, rubber spatula, long serrated knife, pastry bag with #1 or #2 star tip

1½ CUPS GRANULATED SUGAR	2 EGG WHITES
1 CUP ALL-PURPOSE FLOUR	1½ CUPS (ABOUT 7½ OUNCES)
2 TEASPOONS BAKING POWDER	HAZELNUTS, TOASTED, SKINNED,
¼ TEASPOON SALT	AND GROUND MEDIUM-FINE (SEE
4 EGGS, SEPARATED	FOOTNOTE ON PAGE 21)
½ CUP VEGETABLE OIL	GANACHE (SEE PAGE 209)
1 TEASPOON VANILLA EXTRACT	CHOCOLATE GLAZE (SEE PAGE 210)

1. Position the rack in the center of the oven and preheat the oven to 350 degrees. Butter or coat with vegetable spray a 10 × 3-inch round baking pan. Dust with flour, inverting the pan and tapping out any excess flour. Set aside.

2. Reserving 2 tablespoons sugar, sift together the sugar, flour, baking powder, and salt. Set aside.

3. In the large bowl of an electric mixer fitted with a paddle or beaters, beat the egg yolks at high speed. Turn the machine to low and pour in the oil and vanilla. On low speed, gradually add the sifted ingredients, then turn up the speed, and beat until well combined and smooth. This may take a few minutes, so be patient.

4. In another clean large bowl, with whip or clean beaters, whip the 6 egg whites until soft peaks form. Start on medium speed and raise the speed as the peaks begin to form. Gradually pour in the reserved 2 tablespoons of sugar and continue to whip until the whites are shiny and firm but not stiff. With a rubber spatula, fold one-quarter of the whites into the egg yolk mixture, then scrape the egg yolk mixture

back into the whites, quickly folding until completely incorporated. Remove the bowl from the mixer and fold in the ground hazelnuts.

5. Scrape into the prepared pan and bake until the cake is golden brown and springs back when lightly touched, about 35 minutes. Cool on a rack.

6. When completely cool, run a sharp knife around the inside edges of the pan, separating the cake from the pan, and invert the pan onto a smooth flat surface. Using a long serrated knife, cut the cake into two or three layers. Saving the best layer for the top, spread a thin layer of Ganache between the layers. (See page 227 on how to prepare and frost a layer cake.) Refrigerate until the frosting sets. Transfer the cake to a rack and fit the rack into a baking tray. Drizzle the glaze over the cake and refrigerate until set. Decorate by piping a latticework pattern of Ganache over the top and a border around the outside edges, or pipe Ganache rosettes decoratively on the top. Remove the cake from the refrigerator 30 minutes before serving.

TO PREPARE AHEAD: Through step 5, the cake can be made 1 day ahead, wrapped well, and refrigerated. Frost and glaze early in the day the cake is being served.

MARBLED POUND CAKE

Makes 1 loaf,
8 1/2 × 3 1/2 × 2 1/2 inches
Serves 10 to 12

We love this versatile cake. If you double the recipe, you can bake it in a 10-inch bundt pan. We've baked it in a loaf pan, cupcake tins, and a bundt pan, and all have turned out beautifully. In the bundt pan, baking time is about 1 1/2 hours, the cupcakes bake in 20 to 25 minutes, and in the loaf pan, baking time is about 1 hour. This is great with a glass of cold milk.

EQUIPMENT: 8 1/2 × 3 1/2 × 2 1/2-inch loaf pan, sifter, electric mixer with large bowl, metal spatula or flat knife, wide spatula

2 CUPS ALL-PURPOSE FLOUR	2 EGGS
1 TEASPOON BAKING SODA	1 CUP BUTTERMILK
1 TEASPOON BAKING POWDER	1 1/2 TEASPOONS VANILLA EXTRACT
1/2 TEASPOON SALT	1/2 CUP UNSWEETENED COCOA
4 OUNCES (1 STICK) UNSALTED BUTTER,	POWDER, SIFTED
AT ROOM TEMPERATURE, CUT INTO	1/2 CUP SEMISWEET CHOCOLATE CHIPS
SMALL PIECES	CHOCOLATE GLAZE (SEE PAGE 210)
1 CUP GRANULATED SUGAR	

1. Position the rack in the center of the oven and preheat the oven to 350 degrees. Butter or coat with vegetable spray an 8 1/2 × 3 1/2 × 2 1/2-inch loaf pan.

2. Sift together the flour, baking soda, baking powder, and salt. Set aside.

3. In the large bowl of an electric mixer fitted with a paddle or beaters, beat the butter on medium speed. Gradually pour in the sugar, raise the speed to high and beat until fluffy. Add the eggs, one at a time, beating just to combine. Turn the speed to low and alternate adding the flour mixture and the buttermilk, starting and ending with the flour mixture (three additions of flour and two of buttermilk). Add the vanilla with the last addition of buttermilk.

4. Scrape two-thirds of the batter into the prepared pan. Add the sifted cocoa to the batter remaining in the bowl, and beat until well blended. Fold in the chocolate

chips. Drop large spoonfuls of the chocolate mixture over the batter in the loaf pan and swirl through the batter with a metal spatula or flat knife, resulting in a marbled effect. Bake until a cake tester gently inserted into the center of the cake comes out clean, about 1 hour. Set on a rack to cool.

5. When completely cool, release the cake from the pan by running a sharp knife around the inside of the pan, separating the cake from the pan, and invert the cake onto a rack. Place a pan below the rack and drizzle the glaze over the cake. Let set. Slip a long heavy spatula under the cake and transfer the cake to a flat surface.

6. To serve, cut a thin slice off both ends* (end pieces are for family consumption) and cut the cake into eight slices. No garnish is needed for this cake, but for color, you can place a strawberry or a sprig of mint alongside each slice.

TO PREPARE AHEAD: Through step 4, the cake can be made 1 day ahead, wrapped well, and finished the next day.

* Since there are no "ends" when baked in a bundt pan or cupcake tins, this may not apply.

CHOCOLATE CRAQUELINE MOUSSE CAKE

Makes one 10-inch cake

Serves 12 to 14

This cake makes frequent appearances on the Spago menu. It is a spectacular cake, not difficult to prepare, and will be a most impressive addition to your repertoire. The craqueline that we use in the restaurant is supplied by large companies in large quantities. However, because craqueline tastes so much like crushed sugar cones, we decided to use the sugar cones for the recipe. Sugar cones can be purchased in many supermarkets.

EQUIPMENT: 10 × 3-inch round cake pan or 10-inch springform pan, medium heatproof bowl, rolling pin, long serrated knife, 10-inch cardboard round, offset spatula, soft pastry brush, long spatula, pastry bag with #3 star tip, wide spatula

CHOCOLATE CHIFFON CAKE (SEE PAGE 13), BAKED IN A 10 × 3-INCH ROUND CAKE PAN

PEANUT BUTTER CRAQUELINE FILLING

5 OUNCES MILK CHOCOLATE, CUT INTO SMALL PIECES

8 SUGAR CONES

½ CUP CREAMY PEANUT BUTTER

. . .

ABOUT ¼ CUP SUGAR SYRUP (SEE PAGE 217)

½ RECIPE CHOCOLATE MOUSSE (SEE PAGE 195) OR MOCHA MOUSSE (SEE PAGE 199), *WITH NO INSTANT COFFEE*

ABOUT 1 CUP GANACHE (SEE PAGE 209)

1. Bake the Chocolate Chiffon Cake as directed in a 10 × 3-inch round cake pan, baking until a cake tester gently inserted into the center of the cake comes out clean, 35 to 40 minutes. Cool on a rack.

2. Make the craqueline filling: In a medium heatproof bowl set over a pan of simmering water, melt the chocolate, stirring occasionally. Meanwhile, enclose the cones in a plastic bag and run a rolling pin over the bag, crushing the cones into very small pieces. Remove the chocolate from the heat, stir in the peanut butter, and then fold in the crushed cones. Set aside.

3. Assemble the cake: With a long serrated knife, cut the cake into three layers (see page 227). Saving the most level layer for the top, set the first layer on a 10-inch

cardboard round. With an offset spatula, spread the craqueline filling over the cake. Set the second layer on the craqueline filling, pressing down gently to secure. With a soft pastry brush, brush the Sugar Syrup over the second layer and then spread the mousse over, leveling with a long clean spatula, making it as smooth as possible. Top with the last layer and refrigerate until the mousse sets, about 30 minutes.

4. When ready to frost, remove the cake from the refrigerator and brush away any excess crumbs from the top of the cake. Using an offset spatula, frost the top of the cake only with the Ganache. (The sides remain unfrosted so that the layering effect is visible.) Spoon the remaining Ganache into a pastry bag fitted with a #3 star tip and decorate the cake with rosettes. Refrigerate until firm, at least 30 minutes. Remove the cake from the refrigerator, run the blade of a long sharp knife under the cake, then slip a wide spatula directly under the cake and transfer to a clean plate. Refrigerate until needed, removing about 30 minutes before serving.

TO PREPARE AHEAD: Through step 3 the cake can be made 1 day ahead. Through step 4, the cake can be assembled early in the day it is to be served.

SMALL CAKES, CRÊPES, AND PASTRIES

CINCO DE MAYO CHOCOLATE-CINNAMON BROWNIES 47

PEANUT BUTTER BROWNIES WITH
TOASTED PEANUTS AND MILK CHOCOLATE 49

HAZELNUT BROWNIES 52

JUDY'S CHOCOLATE-DATE CAKE 54

PEANUT BUTTER BARS 56

MADELEINES AU CHOCOLAT 59

CHOCOLATE-CHOCOLATE CUPCAKES 61

HAZELNUT DOMES 63

CHOCOLATE CRÊPES
WITH TOASTED ALMOND CREAM AND CARAMELIZED PEARS 66

GINGER CRÊPES WITH CHOCOLATE ZABAIONE 69

PÂTE SUCRÉE 71

CHOCOLATE PÂTE SUCRÉE 72

CHOCOLATE BRIOCHE 73

a comfort food makes you feel good with the very first bite. Though each of the cakes in this chapter fits into that "comfort zone," one dessert tops everyone's list of favorites: the chocolate brownie.

When Spago Las Vegas was opening, Mary had to design two pastry menus: elegant desserts for the dining room, more rustic and familiar ones for the café. The day before the restaurant opened, Wolfgang took Mary aside and told her that he was concerned about one of her decisions—putting a brownie sundae on the café menu. Brownies hadn't been on a Spago menu before. Mary had only made them for the staff. Whenever there was a plateful in the kitchen, Wolfgang would pick up a brownie and say, "What are these chocolate squares you Americans like?" Imagine his chagrin when he learned that not only was the sundae one of the most asked-for desserts, but Random House had selected the Best-Ever Brownie Sundae for the cover of our first dessert book!

The pastries in this chapter are traditional recipes modified with our kitchen experience. They can be doubled, cut into portions, and frozen, so that you can have any one of them at a moment's notice.

Some people are intimidated at the prospect of making crêpes, but be reassured; there's no mystery in producing a delicate, paper-thin crêpe. It's quite easy and well worth the effort.

. . .

CINCO DE MAYO CHOCOLATE-CINNAMON BROWNIES

Serves 8

The addition of cayenne gives this brownie a little "bite." Try it! We think you'll like it. To make a fun Cinco de Mayo dessert, arrange one of the brownies on a small plate, top with a scoop of vanilla ice cream, and sprinkle finely chopped *caheta*, a Mexican candy, over.*

EQUIPMENT: 8-inch round cake pan, small baking tray, sifter, large heatproof bowl, whisk, 8-inch cardboard round

½ CUP (2½ OUNCES) PINE NUTS

½ CUP ALL-PURPOSE FLOUR

½ TEASPOON GROUND CINNAMON

½ TEASPOON SALT

¼ TEASPOON CAYENNE PEPPER, OPTIONAL

8 OUNCES UNSWEETENED CHOCOLATE,
    CUT INTO SMALL PIECES

4 OUNCES (1 STICK) UNSALTED BUTTER,
    CUT INTO SMALL PIECES

1 CUP DARK BROWN SUGAR, FIRMLY
    PACKED

½ CUP GRANULATED SUGAR

2 EGGS, LIGHTLY WHISKED

1 TEASPOON VANILLA EXTRACT

1. Position the rack in the center of the oven and preheat the oven to 350 degrees. Lightly butter or spray with vegetable spray an 8-inch round cake pan. Set aside.

2. Spread the nuts in a small baking tray and toast in the oven until golden brown, 7 to 8 minutes, turning the nuts with a spatula halfway through cooking time. Set aside.

3. Sift together the flour, cinnamon, salt, and cayenne. Set aside.

4. In a large heatproof bowl, combine the pieces of chocolate, the butter, and the brown and granulated sugars. Set the bowl over a pan of simmering water and heat, stirring occasionally, until the chocolate and the butter are almost melted and the sugars have dissolved. Turn off the heat and let continue to melt, stirring as needed.

5. When completely melted, remove the bowl and whisk in the eggs and vanilla. Fold in the flour mixture, then the pine nuts. Scrape into the prepared pan and bake until the cake springs back when pressed lightly, about 25 minutes. Cool on a rack. To remove from the pan, run the tip of a sharp knife around the inside of pan, loosening

* *Caheta* usually can be found in markets where Mexican products are sold.

the cake from the pan, and invert the cake onto a rack. Place an 8-inch cardboard round on top of the cake and invert the cake onto the round.

6. To serve, cut the cake into thin wedges and top with a dollop of whipped cream flavored with a little vanilla.

TO PREPARE AHEAD: Through step 5, cake can be made 1 day ahead.

PEANUT BUTTER BROWNIES WITH TOASTED PEANUTS AND MILK CHOCOLATE

Makes nine 2½-inch squares

This is the ideal dessert for those of us who can never get enough of a good thing. It can also be served with ice cream and hot fudge.

EQUIPMENT: 8-inch square baking pan, sifter, medium heatproof bowl, electric mixer with large bowl, rubber spatula, small metal spatula

2 CUPS ALL-PURPOSE FLOUR

1 TEASPOON BAKING POWDER

½ TEASPOON SALT

8 OUNCES (2 STICKS) UNSALTED BUTTER, AT ROOM TEMPERATURE, CUT INTO SMALL PIECES

4 OUNCES BITTERSWEET CHOCOLATE, COARSELY CHOPPED

2 CUPS DARK BROWN SUGAR, FIRMLY PACKED

2 EGGS

1 TEASPOON VANILLA EXTRACT

1 CUP CHUNKY PEANUT BUTTER

8 OUNCES UNSALTED PEANUTS, TOASTED (SEE FOOTNOTE ON PAGE 21), AND COARSELY CHOPPED

8 OUNCES MILK CHOCOLATE, COARSELY CHOPPED

1. Position the rack in the center of the oven and preheat the oven to 350 degrees. Butter or coat with vegetable spray an 8-inch square baking pan. Dust with flour, tapping out any excess. Set aside.

2. Sift together the flour, baking powder, and salt. Set aside.

3. In a medium heatproof bowl set over a pan of simmering water, melt 4 tablespoons (2 ounces) butter and the bittersweet chocolate until almost melted, stirring occasionally. Remove from the heat and let melt completely.

4. In the large bowl of an electric mixer fitted with a paddle or beaters, beat together the remaining 6 ounces of butter and the sugar. Start on low speed until the sugar is incorporated, then raise the speed to high and beat until fluffy, stopping the mixer occasionally and scraping down the sides of the bowl and under the beaters as necessary with a rubber spatula. Turn the speed to medium and add the eggs, one at a

time, the peanut butter, and the vanilla. Scrape in the melted chocolate mixture and beat until thoroughly incorporated.

5. Turn the speed to low, add the flour mixture, and beat until just combined. Add the peanuts and milk chocolate, and again beat just until combined.

6. Scrape the batter into the prepared pan and level with a small metal spatula. Bake until the top is firm to the touch and a cake tester gently inserted into the center of the cake comes out clean, 40 to 45 minutes, turning the cake front to back after 20 minutes. Cool on a rack.

7. When completely cool, using a sharp knife, run the knife around the inside edges of the baking pan, separating the cake from the pan. Invert the cake onto a rack and then back onto a firm, flat surface. Carefully cut away the hard outside edges of the cake. Cut the cake into 9 pieces, each piece about $2\frac{1}{2}$ inches square.

8. Serve as is or with softly whipped cream, or as suggested above, as part of a sundae.

TO PREPARE AHEAD: Through step 6 or 7, the cake can be prepared 1 day ahead.

HAZELNUT BROWNIES

Makes 36 brownies

This is a lusciously rich, moist brownie, soft on the inside and chewy on the outside. Hazelnut oil is expensive, but it definitely adds to the flavor of the brownie. Purchase the smallest quantity available. This was baked in a heavy-duty aluminum pan with a removable bottom.*

EQUIPMENT: 9-inch square baking pan, small baking tray, medium and large heat-proof bowls, sifter, whisk, electric mixer with large bowl

HAZELNUT PASTE
5 OUNCES HAZELNUTS
2 TABLESPOONS HAZELNUT OIL

BROWNIE
¾ POUND BITTERSWEET CHOCOLATE,
    CUT INTO SMALL PIECES
8 OUNCES (2 STICKS) UNSALTED BUTTER,
    AT ROOM TEMPERATURE, CUT INTO
    SMALL PIECES

1½ CUPS ALL-PURPOSE FLOUR
1 TEASPOON BAKING POWDER
½ TEASPOON SALT
4 EGGS
2 CUPS GRANULATED SUGAR
1 TEASPOON VANILLA EXTRACT

1. Position the rack in the center of the oven and preheat the oven to 350 degrees. Butter or coat with vegetable spray a 9-inch square baking pan. Dust with flour, tapping out any excess flour. Set aside.

2. Make the hazelnut paste: Spread the nuts on a small baking tray and toast in the oven, 10 to 12 minutes, turning the nuts after 5 or 6 minutes. Enclose the nuts in a clean towel and rub until as much of the skin as possible comes off. Cool. Place the hazelnuts in a food processor fitted with a steel blade and process until chopped very fine. Add the oil and continue to process until a paste forms.

3. Make the brownies: In a medium heatproof bowl placed over a pan of simmering water, melt the chocolate and butter. When almost melted, turn off the heat and stir occasionally until completely melted. Stir in the hazelnut paste.

* The pan is available at Williams-Sonoma.

4. Sift together the flour, baking powder, and salt. Set aside.

5. In a large heatproof bowl set over a pan of simmering water, whisk the eggs, sugar, and vanilla until the sugar dissolves. Transfer to the large bowl of an electric mixer fitted with a paddle or beaters, and on high speed beat until pale yellow and quite thick, about 8 minutes. Lower the speed to medium, scrape in the chocolate mixture, and beat until well combined. Stop the machine, pour the flour mixture around the batter, and beat on low speed until just incorporated. Scrape into the prepared pan.

6. Bake until the edges of the cake begin to pull away from the sides of the pan and the top is slightly firm to the touch, 45 to 50 minutes, turning the cake front to back after 25 minutes. Cool on a rack. When cool, run the blade of a sharp knife around the inside edges of the pan, separating the cake from the pan. Invert the cake onto a firm flat surface and cut away any hard edges.

7. To serve, cut the cake into 9 squares, each 3 × 3 inches. Cut each square in half one way (1 1/2 × 3 inches) and then cut the 3-inch length in half. You will have 36 brownies, each 1 1/2 × 1 1/2 inches. To serve, dust the tops of the brownies with sifted confectioners' sugar or serve as is.

TO PREPARE AHEAD: Through step 7, the brownies can be prepared 1 day ahead.

JUDY'S CHOCOLATE-DATE CAKE

Makes eight 2 x 4-inch pieces
or sixteen 2-inch squares

Judy's kids love this cake, and it's a big hit with the Spago "kids" as well. It is a very moist cake that can be cut into small squares for the family or into larger portions, dusted with confectioners' sugar, and served to guests. Some markets sell date nuggets, which can be used instead of the dried dates.

EQUIPMENT: 8-inch square baking pan, small bowl, food processor, sifter, rubber spatula

1 CUP *PITTED* DATES, CUT INTO SMALL
    PIECES

1 TEASPOON BAKING SODA

1 CUP BOILING WATER

1¾ CUPS ALL-PURPOSE FLOUR

2 TABLESPOONS UNSWEETENED COCOA
    POWDER

¼ TEASPOON SALT

6 OUNCES (1½ STICKS) UNSALTED BUTTER,
    CHILLED, CUT INTO SMALL PIECES

1 CUP GRANULATED SUGAR

2 EGGS

1 TEASPOON VANILLA EXTRACT

6 OUNCES (ABOUT 1 CUP) BITTERSWEET OR
    SEMISWEET CHOCOLATE CHIPS

1. Position the rack in the center of the oven and preheat the oven to 350 degrees. Butter or coat with vegetable spray an 8-inch square baking pan. Dust with flour, tapping out any excess flour.

2. Place the cut dates in a small bowl, sprinkle with the baking soda, and pour the boiling water over. Let sit for about 10 minutes, pour into the workbowl of a food processor fitted with a steel blade, and puree, starting with on/off turns and then allowing the machine to run until the dates are pureed. Scrape back into the small bowl and set aside. (Workbowl does not need to be cleaned at this point.)

3. Sift together the flour, cocoa, and salt. Set aside.

4. Using the food processor fitted with a steel blade, cream the butter and sugar, scraping down the sides of the workbowl as necessary. Add the eggs, one at a time, and vanilla, and process just until combined. Add the reserved date mixture and process with on/off turns.

5. Distribute the flour mixture evenly around the workbowl and process with on/off turns until combined. Add half the chocolate chips (3 ounces) and again process with on/off turns just until combined.

6. Using a rubber spatula, scrape the batter into the prepared pan and level by running the spatula over the top of the cake. Sprinkle the remaining chocolate chips over the surface of the cake. Bake 40 to 45 minutes, turning the cake front to back after 20 minutes. The center will not be firm but will become firm while cooling. Cool on a rack.

7. To serve, with a long sharp knife, cut around the inside of the baking pan, separating the cake from the pan. Invert onto a clean flat surface and cut away any hard edges. Turn right side up and cut into the desired number of pieces. Dust with sifted confectioners' sugar. To make it somewhat of a company dessert, place a slice of cake on individual plates, spoon a dollop of whipped cream or ice cream next to it, and garnish with a few berries.

TO PREPARE AHEAD: Through step 6, the cake can be made 1 day ahead and will keep up to 3 days wrapped well in plastic wrap.

PEANUT BUTTER BARS

Makes twenty 3-inch squares

We serve this Spago favorite with Almond Ice Cream with Chocolate-Dipped Almonds (see page 165) and warm Ganache (see page 209), but these squares taste good no matter how you serve them.

EQUIPMENT: 11 x 15 x 1-inch baking tray, sifter, electric mixer with large bowl, rubber spatula, long metal spatula

2 CUPS ALL-PURPOSE FLOUR

1½ TEASPOONS BAKING POWDER

¼ TEASPOON SALT

8 OUNCES (2 STICKS) UNSALTED BUTTER, AT ROOM TEMPERATURE, CUT INTO SMALL PIECES

¾ CUP GRANULATED SUGAR

¾ CUP LESS 2 TABLESPOONS DARK BROWN SUGAR, FIRMLY PACKED

1 CUP CREAMY OR CHUNKY PEANUT BUTTER

3 EGGS

½ TEASPOON VANILLA EXTRACT

6 OUNCES (ABOUT 1 CUP) BITTERSWEET OR SEMISWEET CHOCOLATE CHIPS

1. Position the rack in the center of the oven and preheat the oven to 350 degrees. Coat with vegetable spray an 11 x 15 x 1-inch baking tray and line with parchment or wax paper. Spray the paper with vegetable spray and sprinkle with flour, inverting the pan and tapping off any excess flour. Set aside.

2. Sift together the flour, baking powder, and salt. Set aside.

3. In the large bowl of an electric mixer fitted with a paddle or beaters, on medium speed soften the butter. Add the granulated and brown sugars, raising the speed to high when the sugars are incorporated, and continue to mix until fluffy, stopping the machine and scraping down the sides of the bowl and under the beaters as necessary with rubber spatula. Lower the speed to medium, add the peanut butter, and beat until well mixed. Add the eggs, one at a time, and the vanilla. Turn the speed to low, gradually pour in the flour mixture, and beat just until combined. Add the chocolate chips, again beating just until combined.

4. Spread the batter into the prepared pan, using a long metal spatula to spread and to level. Bake until a cake tester gently poked into the center of the cake comes out clean, 25 to 30 minutes, turning the baking tray back to front after 13 or 14 minutes. Cool on a rack.

5. When cool, invert the baking tray with the cake onto a firm flat surface, separating the cake from the pan. Carefully peel away the paper. Using a long sharp knife, trim the edges of the cake as necessary, then cut into twenty 3-inch squares, turning each square right side up as cut.

6. To serve, place one square on a dessert plate. Arrange a second square so that one of the ends touches the center of the first square. Top with ice cream of your choice and spoon chocolate sauce over. Garnish with a sprig of mint and sprinkle a few raspberries around the cakes. Serve immediately, passing additional sauce.

TO PREPARE AHEAD: Through step 5, the bars can be made 1 day ahead.

MADELEINES AU CHOCOLAT

Makes 28 to 30 large or
55 to 60 small cakes

Madeleines were made famous by the French novelist Marcel Proust. In his *In Search of Lost Time,* a bite of madeleine evokes memories of the narrator's cherished boyhood. We have varied the classic madeleine by adding chocolate, and we feel certain that after one bite you will have your own exquisite memories.

Madeleine pans have grooves in them, which makes it very important to coat them well before filling. We recommend using vegetable spray because it easily coats the grooves. If you prefer, use softened or melted butter.

EQUIPMENT: 1 or 2 large madeleine pans, sifter, medium heatproof bowl, wooden spoon, electric mixer with large bowl

1¼ **CUPS CONFECTIONERS' SUGAR, PLUS EXTRA TO SIFT OVER FINISHED MADELEINES**	4 **OUNCES (1 STICK) UNSALTED BUTTER, CUT INTO PIECES**
1 **CUP ALL-PURPOSE FLOUR**	2 **TEASPOONS GRAND MARNIER, OPTIONAL***
½ **TEASPOON SALT**	1 **TEASPOON VANILLA EXTRACT**
6 **OUNCES BITTERSWEET CHOCOLATE, CUT INTO SMALL PIECES**	5 **LARGE EGG WHITES**

1. Position the rack in the center of the oven and preheat the oven to 400 degrees. Butter or coat with vegetable spray 12 madeleine molds,** making certain that the indentations are well coated. (Or, if you have two pans, spray all 24 molds.)

2. Sift together the sugar, flour, and salt. Set aside.

3. In a medium heatproof bowl set over a pan of simmering water, melt together the chocolate and butter, stirring occasionally with a wooden spoon. When almost

---

* If you want just the orange flavor, 1 teaspoon of finely grated orange rind can be stirred into the cooled chocolate, eliminating the Grand Marnier. (Grated orange rind can also be used *with* the Grand Marnier.)

** If baking small madeleines (1½ × 1 inch), bake about 7 minutes.

melted, remove from the heat and let melt completely. Stir in the Grand Marnier and vanilla until smooth.

4. In the large bowl of an electric mixer fitted with whip or beaters, on medium speed whip the egg whites until frothy. Turn the speed to high and continue to beat until the whites thicken and hold their shape. The whites do not have to be stiff. Fold in the chocolate mixture, blending thoroughly, then fold in the sugar mixture, just until incorporated.

5. Spoon the batter into the prepared molds, filling almost to the top. Bake until the top springs back when lightly touched, about 10 minutes, reversing the baking pan(s) back to front after 5 minutes. Do not overbake. Transfer the pan(s) to a rack, let rest about 5 minutes, then turn the madeleines out onto the rack to cool completely. (If reusing one pan, wash, dry, and respray. Stir through the batter before refilling the molds.)

6. To serve, sift confectioners' sugar over the madeleines just before serving.

TO PREPARE AHEAD: The cakes should be served warm—from the oven to the table. If that isn't convenient, they can be made 1 or 2 hours ahead.

CHOCOLATE-CHOCOLATE CUPCAKES

Makes 12 large cupcakes

Who didn't adore chocolate cupcakes with cream filling when they were kids? Well, this is the adult version . . . rich, melting chocolate on the inside, sinfully good! If these are served warm, do not bake them in paper or foil cups. Just dust with confectioners' sugar and serve, maybe with a small scoop of whipped cream.

EQUIPMENT: 12-cup muffin pan, each cup $2\frac{3}{4} \times 1\frac{1}{4}$ inches, sifter, electric mixer with large bowl

1¼ **CUPS ALL-PURPOSE FLOUR**	1 **CUP GRANULATED SUGAR**
¼ **CUP UNSWEETENED COCOA POWDER**	3 **EGGS**
¼ **TEASPOON SALT**	1 **TEASPOON VANILLA EXTRACT**
⅛ **TEASPOON BAKING SODA**	½ **TEASPOON GRATED ORANGE ZEST**
4 **OUNCES (1 STICK) UNSALTED BUTTER,**	½ **CUP SOUR CREAM**
AT ROOM TEMPERATURE, CUT INTO	4 **OUNCES MILK CHOCOLATE, CUT INTO**
SMALL PIECES	**THICK CHUNKS**

1. Position the rack in the center of the oven and preheat the oven to 350 degrees. Butter or coat with vegetable spray 12 large muffin cups. Set aside. (Muffins can also be baked in paper-cup-lined muffin tins, if desired.)

2. Sift together the flour, cocoa, salt, and baking soda. Set aside.

3. In the large bowl of an electric mixer fitted with a paddle or beaters, on medium speed soften the butter. Gradually add the sugar, turn the speed to high, and continue to beat until fluffy.

4. Add the eggs, one at a time, then the vanilla and orange zest. Beat until well incorporated.

5. Alternate adding the flour mixture and sour cream, starting and ending with the flour mixture (three additions of flour and two of sour cream).

6. Spoon some of the batter into the prepared muffin pan, filling each cup only halfway up. Divide the chunks of milk chocolate and place a few pieces in the center of each

cup. Scrape in the remaining batter, filling almost to the top of each cup. Bake 25 minutes. Do not overbake. Set the pan on a rack for about 5 minutes, then remove the cupcakes to the rack to cool. When completely cool, sprinkle with finely chopped orange zest, if desired, or dust with sifted confectioners' sugar.

TO PREPARE AHEAD: Through step 6, the cupcakes can be made early in the day.

HAZELNUT DOMES

For the Spago 1996 New Year's Eve celebration, we made these and sprinkled the tops with edible gold dust. When they were all lined up on a tray, they looked like the golden domes of the skyline in Venice at sunset.

EQUIPMENT: 12 × 17 × 1-inch baking tray, long offset spatula, 2½-inch cookie cutter, pastry bag with #4 plain tip, flat plate or board

½ **RECIPE HAZELNUT CHIFFON CAKE** **(SEE PAGE 37)** **CHOCOLATE-HAZELNUT MOUSSE** **(SEE PAGE 197)**	**ABOUT 1 CUP CHOCOLATE GLAZE** **(SEE PAGE 210)** ½ **CUP TOASTED HAZELNUTS, CHOPPED** **FINE (SEE FOOTNOTE ON PAGE 21)**

1. Make the Hazelnut Chiffon Cake: Position the rack in the center of the oven and preheat the oven to 350 degrees. Butter or coat with vegetable spray a 12 × 17 × 1-inch baking tray and line with parchment paper. Butter or spray the paper, and dust with flour, inverting the tray and tapping to remove any excess flour.

2. Spread the batter over the prepared pan and even the top by running a long offset spatula across the surface. Bake until the cake is golden and springs back when lightly touched, 12 to 15 minutes. Cool on a rack.

3. When completely cool, with a sharp knife, cut around the edges of the cake, separating the cake from the pan. Invert the tray over a flat firm surface and release the cake. Gently peel away the parchment paper. If the edges of the cake are too hard, cut them away. Using a 2½-inch cookie cutter, cut out 24 circles and arrange them on a rack placed in a clean baking tray. You are going to pipe the mousse over, so make sure that there is enough room between each circle of cake for you to be comfortable while piping. Using a pastry bag fitted with a #4 plain tip, pipe out a large dollop of mousse on top of each circle, forming a mound. To do this, hold the bag upright, close to the cake, and press out the mousse, lifting the tip slightly as the dome gets higher. (If you find it difficult to pipe through the tip, a coarsely chopped nut may have clogged the opening. If that happens, simply poke a long skewer

through the opening, remove the culprit, and continue to pipe.) The finished mound will remind you of a *giant* Hershey Kiss (see photo, page 64). Refrigerate overnight.

4. Glaze the cakes: The next day, remelt the Chocolate Glaze in a small deep pan. Remove the cakes from the refrigerator. Invert each cake and carefully dip each mound of mousse into the warm glaze, just covering the mousse, allowing the cake to show. As each cake is glazed, set it on the rack, so that any excess glaze will drip off onto the tray. Refrigerate 20 to 30 minutes. You want the chocolate to be slightly firm, but still soft enough so that the chopped nuts will adhere to the chocolate.

5. Spread the chopped hazelnuts on a flat plate or board. Roll the sides of each cake into the nuts, coating lightly, and arrange on a large platter. Or place one or two cakes on individual cake plates. Garnish with fresh raspberries strewn around the cakes.

TO PREPARE AHEAD: In step 5, roll the domes in the chopped hazelnuts and refrigerate until needed. Remove from the refrigerator about 30 minutes before serving.

CHOCOLATE CRÊPES WITH TOASTED ALMOND CREAM AND CARAMELIZED PEARS

Makes fifteen to sixteen
6-inch crêpes

We have discovered a miraculously simple way to make crêpes without burning your fingers or tearing the crêpes. The trick is to use two pans, one slightly larger than the crêpe pan. When one side is done, slide it into the second pan and then flip it back into the crêpe pan. With a little practice, you'll find it can be done easily. You can also use just one pan and a spatula. After the first crêpe, your technique will begin to improve, and so will your crêpes! The batter should have the texture of light cream.

EQUIPMENT: sifter, medium bowl, whisk, 7-inch nonstick crêpe pan, small pastry brush, 1-ounce measure or a large spoon equivalent to 2 tablespoons

3 TABLESPOONS ALL-PURPOSE FLOUR

3 TABLESPOONS UNSWEETENED COCOA
  POWDER

3 TABLESPOONS GRANULATED SUGAR

1/4 TEASPOON SALT

3 EGGS

3/4 CUP MILK

5 OR 6 TABLESPOONS CLARIFIED*
  UNSALTED BUTTER

1 TEASPOON VANILLA EXTRACT

1 1/2 TEASPOONS GRATED ORANGE ZEST,
  CHOPPED FINE

TOASTED ALMOND PASTRY CREAM
  (SEE PAGE 203)

CARAMELIZED PEARS**

1. Sift together the flour, cocoa, sugar, and salt. Set aside.

* To clarify butter, over medium heat, melt the butter, remove from the heat and let stand until the foam that forms on top begins to separate from the yellow liquid below, about 20 minutes. Spoon off the foam and then spoon the yellow liquid into a clean jar. This can be refrigerated, covered until needed. Discard the whey that remains on the bottom of the pan. Clarified butter will keep 2 to 3 weeks refrigerated and can be frozen as well.

** To caramelize pears, peel, core, and cut into quarters about 2 pounds of pears. Cut each quarter into 1/2-inch-thick slices. In a large skillet melt 4 tablespoons of butter and arrange the pear slices in the skillet. Sprinkle 1/2 cup granulated sugar over the pears and sauté over medium-high heat until lightly caramelized and tender, turning often so that the pears cook as evenly as possible, 10 to 12 minutes, depending on the ripeness of the pears. Pour in 2 tablespoons of pear brandy, if desired, and cook until the alcohol burns off. (If the alcohol ignites, place a cover over the pan for a few seconds, which will snuff out the flame.) Pour in 1/4 cup heavy cream, stir through, and cook 1 or 2 minutes longer. Keep warm.

2. In a medium bowl, whisk the eggs and milk. Whisk in 3 tablespoons of the clarified butter and the vanilla. Whisk in the flour mixture, whisking until the batter is smooth. Strain into a clean bowl, whisk in the orange zest, and let rest 20 minutes. Stir before making the crêpes.

3. To make the crêpes, heat a 7-inch nonstick crêpe pan and then brush lightly with clarified butter. Using a 1-ounce measure, pour the batter into the pan, immediately tilting the pan so that the bottom of the pan is completely covered with the batter. Over medium heat, cook the crêpe about 30 seconds. The crêpe should be lightly browned, but it may be difficult to see. Shake the pan a few times to loosen the crêpe and then turn it over, using the method suggested above in the headnote, or with a nonstick spatula, and cook about 20 seconds longer. As the crêpes are cooked, transfer to a parchment-lined pan or platter to cool. Do not stack. Repeat with the remaining batter, buttering the crêpe pan as necessary.

4. To serve, arrange a crêpe on a dessert plate and spread 1 heaping tablespoon of the pastry cream down the center of the crêpe. You can fold the crêpe in half, roll the crêpe, enclosing the filling, or fold the sides of the crêpe toward the center and invert onto the plate. Sprinkle with sifted confectioners' sugar and garnish with the caramelized pears topped with a dollop of whipped cream.

TO PREPARE AHEAD: Through step 3, crêpes can be made 1 day ahead. When the crêpes are cool, you can stack them with parchment or wax paper between the crêpes, then wrap the entire stack in plastic wrap or wax paper, then with aluminum foil. Crêpes can also be frozen and defrosted (still wrapped) overnight in the refrigerator. When ready to serve, place the crêpes in a foil package and heat in a 325-degree oven until warm to the touch, 10 to 15 minutes.

GINGER CRÊPES WITH CHOCOLATE ZABAIONE

Makes twenty-four 6-inch crêpes

Mary went to New York a few years ago to teach a high school class how to make crêpes. The kids were a little intimidated at first, but when she showed them how simple it could be, they warmed up to the task. Just remember, your first crêpe in every batch is like your first pancake; it never comes out perfectly. After that, there should be no problem. The most important thing in making crêpes is that you need a good nonstick pan.

EQUIPMENT: sifter, large bowl, whisk, 7-inch nonstick crêpe pan, pastry brush, 1-ounce ladle or ⅛-cup measuring cup

⅔ **CUP ALL-PURPOSE FLOUR**	**5 TABLESPOONS CLARIFIED BUTTER (SEE**
¼ **CUP GRANULATED SUGAR**	**FOOTNOTE, PAGE 66)**
2 TEASPOONS GROUND GINGER	**SPAGO CHOCOLATE ZABAIONE (SEE PAGE**
¼ **TEASPOON SALT**	**146) OR CHOCOLATE MOUSSE (SEE**
4 EGGS	**PAGE 195)**
1 CUP PLUS 2 TABLESPOONS MILK	

1. Sift together the flour, sugar, ginger, and salt. Set aside.

2. In a large bowl, whisk the eggs. Slowly pour in the milk and 2 tablespoons of the clarified butter, and whisk until well combined. Whisk in the flour mixture until smooth. Strain into a clean bowl and let the batter rest 20 minutes. Whisk again before making the crêpes.

3. Heat a nonstick 7-inch crêpe pan and brush lightly with clarified butter. Using a ⅛-cup measuring cup or 1-ounce ladle, pour the batter into the pan and immediately tilt the pan so that the bottom of the pan is completely covered with the batter. Over medium heat, cook the crêpe until lightly browned, about 30 seconds. Shake the pan a few times to loosen the crêpe, and then turn, using a nonstick spatula or a slightly larger pan (see the headnote on page 66). Cook about 20 seconds longer. As the crêpes are cooked, transfer to a parchment-lined pan or plate to cool. Do not stack. Repeat with the remaining batter, brushing the crêpe pan with clarified butter as necessary.

4. To serve, arrange the crêpe on a dessert plate and spread 1 heaping tablespoon of the zabaione or mousse on the crêpe. Fold the crêpe in half or roll the crêpe, enclosing the filling, or fold the sides of the crêpe toward the center and invert onto a plate. Sprinkle sifted confectioners' sugar over the crêpe and garnish with a few fresh berries.

TO PREPARE AHEAD: Through step 3, crêpes can be made 1 day ahead. When the crêpes are cool, you can stack them with parchment or wax paper between the crêpes, then wrap the entire stack in plastic wrap or wax paper, then with aluminum foil. Crêpes can also be frozen and defrosted (still wrapped) overnight in the refrigerator. When ready to serve, place the crêpes in a foil package and heat in a 325-degree oven until warm to the touch, 10 to 15 minutes.

PÂTE SUCRÉE

Makes 1 1/2 pounds
Enough for two 8- or
9-inch pastry shells

Pâte sucrée means "sugar dough." It is a very basic pastry, simple to prepare, and it can be cut into portions and frozen. We use this dough for a variety of tarts, cheesecake bottoms, and sandwich cookies.

EQUIPMENT: food processor, small cup or bowl

2 1/3 CUPS ALL-PURPOSE FLOUR

1/3 CUP GRANULATED SUGAR

8 OUNCES (2 STICKS) UNSALTED BUTTER,
　CHILLED AND CUT INTO SMALL PIECES

2 EGG YOLKS

1 TO 2 TABLESPOONS HEAVY CREAM

1. Using a food processor fitted with a steel blade, combine the flour and sugar with one or two on/off turns. Add the butter and process until the texture resembles fine meal.

2. In a small cup or bowl, using a fork, whisk together the egg yolks and 1 tablespoon cream. Scrape into the food processor and process until a ball begins to form, using the additional cream as necessary. Remove the dough from the machine and wrap in plastic wrap. Refrigerate for at least 3 hours, up to 24 hours, before rolling.

3. Use as needed.

TO PREPARE AHEAD: Through step 2, the Pâte Sucrée can be cut into portions, wrapped well, and frozen.

CHOCOLATE PÂTE SUCRÉE

Makes 1 pound 12 ounces

Enough for two 8-inch tarts

Chocolate Pâte Sucrée can not only be used as a pie or tart crust, but it makes delicious cookies and cakes. It is a bit more difficult to judge when the chocolate crust is done because of the color, so be especially careful not to overbake.

EQUIPMENT: food processor, small cup or bowl, whisk

2 CUPS ALL-PURPOSE FLOUR
1 CUP GRANULATED SUGAR
½ CUP UNSWEETENED COCOA POWDER
6 OUNCES (1½ STICKS) UNSALTED BUTTER,
    CHILLED AND CUT INTO 1-OUNCE
    PIECES

2 EGG YOLKS
2 TABLESPOONS HEAVY CREAM

1. Using a food processor fitted with a steel blade, combine the flour, sugar, and cocoa with a few on/off turns. Arrange the pieces of butter around the blade and process just until combined.

2. In a small cup or bowl, whisk together the egg yolks and cream. With the processor running, pour through the feed tube, making certain you scrape out all the liquid from the cup. Let the machine run until the dough begins to come together, about 1 minute.

3. Scrape the dough out of the processor onto plastic wrap and flatten into a round. Wrap securely and refrigerate for at least 2 to 3 hours, preferably overnight. Use as needed.

TO PREPARE AHEAD: Through step 3, Chocolate Pâte Sucrée can be refrigerated 2 to 3 days, and frozen 2 to 3 weeks. Defrost, wrapped, overnight in the refrigerator.

CHOCOLATE BRIOCHE

Makes 2 loaves, 18 ounces each

At Spago, we use this as an ingredient in the Chocolate Trifle (see page 158). But on its own, Chocolate Brioche is delicious toasted and spread with strawberry jam or orange marmalade.

We use a Dutch-process cocoa and a good milk chocolate (Lindt). Also, because the fresh yeast works better than the dry yeast, we recommend using it. But dry yeast will work if you allow enough time for the rising process. In cold weather, it will take a longer time to rise, sometimes up to 3 hours. A heavy-duty mixer is needed for this bread.

EQUIPMENT: sifter, electric mixer with large bowl, small heatproof bowl, large bowl, 1 or 2 loaf pans, 9 × 5½ × 2½ inches, rolling pin, pastry brush

3½ CUPS ALL-PURPOSE FLOUR	4 LARGE EGGS
⅓ CUP UNSWEETENED COCOA POWDER	¼ CUP COLD WATER
¼ CUP PLUS 2 TABLESPOONS GRANULATED SUGAR	7 OUNCES (1¾ STICKS) UNSALTED BUTTER, AT ROOM TEMPERATURE, CUT INTO SMALL PIECES
2 TEASPOONS TABLE SALT (NOT KOSHER SALT)	2 OUNCES MILK CHOCOLATE, CUT INTO SMALL PIECES
0.6 OUNCES FRESH YEAST OR 2 TABLESPOONS (2 PACKAGES) DRY YEAST	1 TABLESPOON HEAVY CREAM

1. Sift the flour, cocoa, and sugar into the large bowl of an electric mixer fitted with a dough hook. Run the machine for 1 or 2 minutes to combine thoroughly. Stop the machine and on one side of the bowl, on top of the mixture, carefully sprinkle the salt. On the opposite side, sprinkle in the yeast. Add the eggs and water, and start the machine, slowly at first, then a little faster, and beat until the dough comes away from the sides of the bowl and clings to the dough hook, about 5 minutes.

2. With the machine running at medium speed, add the butter, one or two pieces at a time. As each addition is absorbed into the dough, add a little more until all the butter is incorporated.

3. Meanwhile, in a small heatproof bowl set over a pan of simmering water, melt the chocolate. Because it is only 2 ounces, heat the bowl, turn off the heat, and let the chocolate melt, stirring occasionally. With the last bit of butter, add the melted

chocolate and continue to beat until the dough is an even chocolate color, stopping the machine and scraping down the sides of the bowl and dough hook as necessary.

4. This is a sticky dough. To make it easier to remove the dough, sprinkle a little flour over the dough in the bowl and then turn out onto a lightly floured surface, dusting your hands with flour as necessary. Gently pat down the dough, flattening it slightly, and fold all four sides toward the center, and meeting in the middle. Place the dough in a large buttered bowl, seam side down, cover with plastic wrap, and refrigerate overnight.

5. When ready to use, divide the dough in half, about 18 ounces each, refrigerating the unused half, covered, until needed.

6. To make the bread, butter a 9 × 5½ × 2½-inch loaf pan and set aside. Preheat the oven to 300 degrees, turn off the oven, and let cool slightly. While the oven is heating, let the dough sit at room temperature.

7. On a lightly floured surface, roll out half the dough to a 7 × 10-inch rectangle. With the 10-inch side in front of you, start rolling the dough. Give it one roll and pinch down on the edges to seal. Roll the outer (7-inch) sides in slightly and continue to roll up the bread. Halfway through, repeat the pinching down along the edges. The dough should be a little shorter than the length of the pan. Place the dough into the prepared pan, seam side down, and set in the turned-off oven, uncovered, until the dough doubles in size, 2 to 3 hours.

8. Remove the pan from the oven and place in a warm spot. Position the rack in the center of the oven and preheat the oven to 325 degrees. With a clean pastry brush, brush the top of the bread with the cream and return the pan to the oven. Bake until the bread is fairly firm to the touch, about 30 minutes, turning the pan front to back after 15 minutes. Do not overbake. Remove to a rack, let cool for 5 minutes, then turn out onto the rack to cool completely and use as needed.

9. Repeat with the remaining dough.

TO PREPARE AHEAD: Through step 4, the bread can be made 1 day ahead. Through step 8, it can be baked the next day. When cool, the bread can be sliced and frozen.

PIES, TARTS, AND CHEESECAKES

MERINGUE NAPOLEON WITH WHITE CHOCOLATE MOUSSE
AND CHOCOLATE MOUSSE 77

SPECTACULAR BOSTON CREAM PIE 80

CHELLE'S BANANA-SOUR CREAM TART 83

CHOCOLATE-NOUGATINE TART WITH APRICOT ICE CREAM
AND WARM APRICOT COMPOTE 85

MILK CHOCOLATE-PISTACHIO TART 88

CHOCOLATE-CHIP CHEESECAKE WITH CHERRY COMPOTE 90

CHOCOLATE CHEESECAKE 92

"COOKIES AND CREAM" CHEESECAKE 95

*F*ruit filling for pies and tarts is fine, but for a serious chocoholic, chocolate-filled pies and tarts are the ultimate indulgence.

One of our favorites is Chelle's Banana–Sour Cream Tart. Mary has taken ordinary ingredients and created a dessert that is both beautiful and delectable. At the restaurant, it is made with the small finger bananas that have a delightfully fruity flavor. However, if these are not available, the larger ones can be used.

The crust that we suggest for each tart can be Pâte Sucrée or Chocolate Pâte Sucrée, which heightens the flavor and makes a more attractive presentation. When it comes to cheesecakes, chocolate is a colorful addition not only to the appearance but definitely to the taste.

Our cheesecakes take a little longer to bake than most desserts because they are baked in a water bath. This helps prevent the cakes from cracking on the top. They also need to be very firm before being sliced and must be refrigerated overnight.

• • •

MERINGUE NAPOLEON WITH WHITE CHOCOLATE MOUSSE AND CHOCOLATE MOUSSE

Serves 8

Imagine white meringue rounds nestled in a pool of red Raspberry Compote. Between the meringues are layers of chocolate and whipped cream. Melted chocolate drizzles down the sides. This is an elegant dessert and probably should be reserved for special occasions. We prepare it with White Chocolate Mousse and Chocolate Mousse, but it can be layered with just one, if desired.

EQUIPMENT: 2 baking trays, electric mixer with large bowl, pastry bag(s) with #4 plain tip, small and wide spatulas, medium heatproof bowl, small piping bag

MERINGUE ROUNDS	CHOCOLATE ROUNDS
4 EGG WHITES	8 OUNCES BITTERSWEET CHOCOLATE
PINCH OF SALT	. . .
¼ TEASPOON CREAM OF TARTAR	1 CUP HEAVY CREAM, WHIPPED
1 CUP GRANULATED SUGAR	2 CUPS WHITE CHOCOLATE MOUSSE
	(SEE PAGE 201), CHOCOLATE MOUSSE
	(SEE PAGE 195), OR MOCHA MOUSSE
	(SEE PAGE 199)
	RASPBERRY COMPOTE (SEE PAGE 216)

1. Make the meringues: On two sheets of parchment or wax paper, draw twenty-four 3-inch circles. Turn the papers over and place on two baking trays. The circles should still be visible.

2. In the large bowl of an electric mixer fitted with a whip or beaters, on medium speed whip the egg whites and salt until frothy. Lower the speed, add the cream of tartar, and gradually pour in the sugar. Turn up the speed to high and beat until the meringue is very thick and very shiny.

3. Position the rack in the center of the oven and preheat the oven to 250 degrees.

4. Fill a large pastry bag fitted with a #4 plain tip with the meringue. Pipe a ring of the meringue around the outer edges of one of the drawn circles. Pipe a second ring inside the first and then fill in the center. With a small spatula, smooth the top as

needed to flatten slightly. Repeat, filling the remaining drawn circles. You will have some meringue left over. Use this to pipe strips of meringue wherever there is some empty space on the paper. The strips will be broken up into pieces, some small and some a little larger, and used as garnish. Bake until the meringues are dry but still white, about 45 minutes. Cool on a rack.

5. Make the chocolate rounds: In a medium heatproof bowl set over a pan of simmering water, melt the chocolate, stirring occasionally. When almost melted, remove from the heat and allow to melt completely.

6. On a sheet of parchment or wax paper, draw sixteen 3-inch circles. Cut out each circle and place the circles on a flat work surface, penciled side down. Spoon 1 tablespoon of the melted chocolate on each circle and, with a small spatula, spread the chocolate evenly over the circle, making certain that the circle is completely covered. Reserve the remaining melted chocolate and reheat when ready to assemble the dessert. With a wide spatula, carefully transfer each chocolate-coated paper circle to a dry baking tray. Refrigerate until set. Then, turn over each circle and gently peel away the paper. Return the chocolate circle to the tray and refrigerate until needed.

7. Assemble the Napoleons: Place 1 meringue circle on a flat surface and top with a chocolate circle. Pipe or spoon whipped cream on the chocolate circle, then top with a second meringue circle and a second chocolate circle. Pipe or spoon Chocolate Mousse on the round of chocolate and top with a third meringue circle. Place the remaining melted chocolate in a small piping bag made with parchment paper (see page 223). Cut a small piece off the tip and pipe chocolate decoratively over the top. Repeat with the remaining meringue circles, chocolate circles, whipped cream, Chocolate Mousse, and melted chocolate.

8. To serve, set each completed Napoleon on a large dessert plate. Spoon Raspberry Compote around the Napoleon and garnish with broken bits of meringue strips. Serve immediately.

TO PREPARE AHEAD: Through step 6, prepare and refrigerate. Have the whipped cream, mousse, and Raspberry Compote ready, and assemble at serving time.

SPECTACULAR BOSTON CREAM PIE

This is the Spago version of Boston cream pie, which is not a pie at all, but rather a layered white cake filled with pastry cream. We start with a double recipe of our Buttermilk Cake, layer it with Chocolate Pastry Cream, and glaze it with a Chocolate Glaze. The recipe can be cut in half and baked in one 9-inch round baking pan, the cake layer then cut in half, frosted, and glazed. Our version is a bit more spectacular and will easily serve a large group.

EQUIPMENT: two 9-inch round cake pans, sifter, electric mixer with large bowl, two 9-inch cardboard rounds, medium heatproof bowl, whisk, fine-mesh strainer, long metal spatula, rack to fit into baking tray, baking tray, large ladle, wide, flat spatula

BUTTERMILK CAKE
3½ CUPS ALL-PURPOSE FLOUR
2 TEASPOONS BAKING POWDER
1 TEASPOON BAKING SODA
1 TEASPOON SALT
1½ CUPS GRANULATED SUGAR
8 OUNCES (2 STICKS) UNSALTED BUTTER,
    AT ROOM TEMPERATURE, CUT INTO
    SMALL PIECES
8 EGG YOLKS
2 CUPS BUTTERMILK

CHOCOLATE GLAZE FOR BOSTON CREAM PIE
8 OUNCES BITTERSWEET CHOCOLATE,
    CUT INTO SMALL PIECES
3 OUNCES (¾ STICK) UNSALTED BUTTER,
    CUT INTO SMALL PIECES
⅓ CUP LIGHT CORN SYRUP

· · ·

CHOCOLATE PASTRY CREAM
(SEE PAGE 193)

1. Make the Buttermilk Cake: Position the rack in the center of the oven and preheat the oven to 350 degrees. Butter or coat with vegetable spray two 9-inch round cake pans. Dust with flour, tapping out any excess flour. Set aside.

2. Sift together the flour, baking powder, baking soda, and salt. Set aside.

3. In the large bowl of an electric mixer fitted with a paddle or beaters, beat the sugar and butter. Start on low speed until slightly blended, then gradually turn to high and beat until fluffy. Add the yolks, one at a time, beating to just combine after each addition. Turn the speed to low, and alternate adding the flour mixture and buttermilk, starting and ending with the flour mixture (three additions of flour and two of buttermilk).

4. Divide the batter between the two prepared pans and gently tap the pans on a work surface to level. Bake until a cake tester gently inserted into the center of the cake comes out clean, about 45 minutes. Transfer the pans to racks and let cool in the pan for 15 minutes. Then invert the cakes onto two 9-inch cardboard rounds and return to the racks to cool completely.

5. Make the glaze: In a medium heatproof bowl set over a pan of simmering water, combine the chocolate and butter. When almost melted, turn off the heat and let continue to melt, stirring occasionally. Whisk in the corn syrup until smooth. Strain through a fine strainer and reserve, covered. The glaze should be kept warm until needed.

6. Assemble the cake: When ready to finish the cake, see page 227 on how to prepare and frost a layer cake. Using a long metal spatula, divide the pastry cream and spread between the layers. Refrigerate and allow to set before glazing.

7. To glaze, fit a cooling rack into a baking tray and place the cake on the rack. With a large ladle, spoon enough of the glaze over the cake to cover the entire top and all the sides. Then *carefully* tilt the baking pan slightly so that any excess glaze will run off the top of the cake. Refrigerate the entire tray with the rack and cake until the glaze is set, about 15 minutes. Remove from the refrigerator. Slide a wide, flat spatula *under* the cardboard round and lift the cake off the rack, returning the cake to the refrigerator until needed. The chocolate that is in the baking tray can be scraped up, wrapped, and stored in the refrigerator.

TO PREPARE AHEAD: Through step 7, the cake can be completed early in the day and refrigerated. Remove from the refrigerator about 10 minutes before serving.

CHELLE'S BANANA-SOUR CREAM TART

Makes one 10-inch tart
Serves 8 to 10

Chelle Meldrum, the unofficial mom and official controller at Spago, was the inspiration for this tart. One day she walked into the pastry kitchen and asked for a banana and a scoop of sour cream, saying that she loved the combination—it was her ultimate comfort food. That's all Mary had to hear. The bananas *must* be ripe; the bitterness of green bananas will overwhelm the taste of the tart.

EQUIPMENT: 10-inch pie plate, with 1½-inch sides, baking tray, rolling pin, sifter, large mixing bowl, whisk

¾ POUND CHOCOLATE PÂTE SUCRÉE (SEE PAGE 72)	**2 CUPS SOUR CREAM**
	1 CUP DARK BROWN SUGAR, FIRMLY PACKED
FILLING	**2 TEASPOONS VANILLA EXTRACT**
½ CUP ALL-PURPOSE FLOUR	**6 OUNCES BITTERSWEET CHOCOLATE, COARSELY CHOPPED**
1 TEASPOON FRESHLY GRATED NUTMEG	
PINCH OF SALT	**4 OR 5 *RIPE* BANANAS (1½ POUNDS)**
2 LARGE EGGS	**½ CUP COARSELY CHOPPED WALNUTS**

1. Position the rack in the center of the oven and preheat the oven to 350 degrees. Coat a 10-inch pie plate (1½ inches deep) with vegetable spray. Line a baking tray with parchment paper. Set aside.

2. Make the tart shell: On a lightly floured work surface, roll out the Chocolate Pâte Sucrée to a 12-inch circle. Arrange on the parchment-lined baking tray and bake until lightly crisp, 20 to 25 minutes. Set aside to cool. (Leave the oven on.) When cool, using a sharp knife and the bottom of the pie plate as a guide, cut out a 10-inch circle and place in the bottom of the pie plate. Break up the remaining shell, loosely wrap in wax paper or a plastic bag, and crush into fine crumbs by rolling a heavy rolling pin over the enclosed crust. Set aside.

3. Make the filling: Sift together the flour, nutmeg, and salt. Set aside.

4. In a large bowl, using a whisk, whip the eggs and sour cream until smooth. Whisk

in the sugar, vanilla, and the flour mixture until well combined. Fold in the coarsely chopped chocolate.

5. Assemble the tart: Cut the bananas into long, thick slices. Arrange the slices on the chocolate crust, covering the entire surface. Sprinkle the walnuts over the bananas and pour the filling into the pie plate. The filling should come to the very top of the pie plate.

6. Place the pie plate on a baking tray for easier handling and bake until the tart feels slightly firm to the touch, about 45 minutes. Remove from the oven. You will notice that the center of the tart is slightly lower than the outer rim. Sprinkle the reserved chocolate crumbs on top, covering only the center of the tart. Place on a rack to cool. Then refrigerate until firm, at least 1 hour. When ready to serve, cut with a sharp knife and remove the slices with a wide pie server.

TO PREPARE AHEAD: Through step 6, the tart should be made early in the day.

SPAGO CHOCOLATE

CHOCOLATE-NOUGATINE TART WITH
APRICOT ICE CREAM AND WARM APRICOT COMPOTE

Serves 8

The crisp pastry, crunchy nougatine, and smooth chocolate filling blend perfectly to make this unusual tart. The Apricot Compote completes the picture.

EQUIPMENT: baking tray, medium saucepan, long-handled wooden spoon, large heavy knife or food processor, rolling pin, tart pan, 10 × 1½ inches, small heatproof bowl, electric mixer with large bowl

NOUGATINE
¾ CUP GRANULATED SUGAR
¼ CUP LIGHT CORN SYRUP
3 OUNCES (1 SCANT CUP) SLICED
    ALMONDS, BLANCHED OR UNBLANCHED
    ...
1 POUND PÂTE SUCRÉE (SEE PAGE 71)
    OR CHOCOLATE PÂTE SUCRÉE (SEE
    PAGE 72)

CHOCOLATE FILLING
5 OUNCES BITTERSWEET CHOCOLATE,
    CUT INTO SMALL PIECES

5 OUNCES (1 STICK PLUS 2 TABLESPOONS)
    UNSALTED BUTTER, CUT INTO SMALL
    PIECES
3 EGGS
3 EGG YOLKS
½ CUP GRANULATED SUGAR
3 TABLESPOONS ALL-PURPOSE FLOUR,
    SIFTED
    ...
APRICOT COMPOTE (SEE PAGE 216)
APRICOT ICE CREAM (SEE PAGE 167),
    OPTIONAL

1. Make the nougatine: Lightly oil or coat with vegetable spray a baking tray. Set aside. In a medium saucepan, combine the sugar and corn syrup. Over medium heat, bring to a boil and cook until caramel colored. Watch carefully, making sure that the caramel doesn't burn.* Immediately add the nuts and stir with a long-handled wooden spoon until well combined. Remove from the heat and spread the nougatine out on the prepared baking tray. When cool, turn out on a firm surface. Divide in half. Using a large heavy knife, chop one half fine, the remaining half into coarse pieces. (Or if you prefer, chop in a food processor fitted with a steel blade, with on/off turns.) Set aside.

---

* Making caramel can be a very sticky proposition, but there is a quick and easy way to dissolve the caramel that sticks to the pot. After pouring it out of the pan, fill the pan with hot water and bring it to a boil. Place your caramel-coated spoon in the pan and continue to boil until the caramel dissolves. Be careful when touching the spoon handle—it will be very hot, so remove it with a potholder. The tart can also be warmed slightly just before serving.

85

2. Roll out the pastry: On a lightly floured surface, flouring the rolling pin and board as necessary, roll out the Pâte Sucrée to about a 12-inch round. Coat a tart pan, 10 × 1½ inches, with vegetable spray. Roll the pastry around the rolling pin and lay it into the pan (if it breaks, just press the pieces together in the pan). Gently press down on the pastry, with your knuckle, fitting it into the bottom and around the sides of the pan. Trim the edges and refrigerate about 20 minutes.

3. Position the rack in the center of the oven and preheat the oven to 350 degrees.

4. Line the chilled pastry with parchment or wax paper and fill to the top with pie weights or beans. Bake 10 minutes, remove the paper and weights, and bake 5 minutes longer. Set aside.

5. Make the filling: In a small heatproof bowl set over a pan of simmering water, melt the chocolate and butter, stirring occasionally. When almost melted, turn off the heat and let melt completely.

6. Meanwhile, in the large bowl of an electric mixer fitted with a paddle or beaters, on high speed beat the eggs, egg yolks, and sugar until very thick and pale yellow, 8 to 10 minutes. Lower the speed and add the flour. When the flour is incorporated, scrape in the chocolate mixture, turn up the speed to medium, and beat until well combined. Stir in the finely chopped nougatine.

7. Pour into the prepared tart shell and bake 20 minutes. Remove from the oven and sprinkle the remaining coarsely chopped nougatine around the top of the tart. Return to the oven and bake until the nougatine is nicely browned, 20 to 25 minutes longer. The top will have puffed but still will not be completely firm. Remove to a rack to cool. As the tart cools, the filling will firm up.

8. To serve, cut the tart into wedges, place each wedge on a dessert plate, and sprinkle with sifted confectioners' sugar. Spoon a little of the Apricot Compote on the side of the tart and place a scoop of Apricot Ice Cream on the compote, if desired. Serve immediately.

TO PREPARE AHEAD: Through step 7, the tart can be made early in the day it is being served. It can be warmed slightly before serving, if desired.

MILK CHOCOLATE–PISTACHIO TART

Makes one 9- or
10-inch tart

Serves 8

In making this tart, we began with a basic pistachio filling. We added milk chocolate, poured it into a tart pan, and, lo and behold—a whole new dessert.

EQUIPMENT: 9- or 10-inch tart pan with removable bottom, rolling pin, food processor, electric mixer with large bowl, rubber spatula, sifter

½ RECIPE CHOCOLATE PÂTE SUCRÉE (SEE PAGE 72), CHILLED

6 OUNCES (ABOUT 1 CUP) SHELLED PISTACHIOS, TOASTED*

¾ CUP GRANULATED SUGAR

6 OUNCES (1½ STICKS) UNSALTED BUTTER, AT ROOM TEMPERATURE, CUT INTO SMALL PIECES

4 EGGS

1 TEASPOON VANILLA EXTRACT

½ TEASPOON ALMOND EXTRACT

¼ CUP ALL-PURPOSE FLOUR, SIFTED

2 OUNCES MILK CHOCOLATE, CUT INTO SMALL PIECES

SIFTED CONFECTIONERS' SUGAR OR GRATED MILK CHOCOLATE

1. Position the rack in the center of the oven and preheat the oven to 350 degrees. Butter or coat with vegetable spray a 9- or 10-inch tart pan with removable bottom.

2. On a lightly floured surface, roll out the chilled dough to a 10-inch circle, about ¼-inch thick. Roll the dough onto a rolling pin and unroll over the prepared tart pan. Gently press down on the dough with your knuckle, shaping it to conform to the bottom and sides of the pan. If the dough breaks, that's okay—just patch together with pieces of dough. Trim the edges by rolling the rolling pin around the top of the pan. Refrigerate while preparing the filling.

3. Using a food processor fitted with a steel blade, combine the cooled, toasted pistachios and sugar. Process until the nuts are finely chopped. Start with on/off turns, then let the machine run for 30 seconds. Stop and check the texture, processing an additional 30 seconds as necessary. Set aside.

* To toast pistachios, spread on a small baking tray and toast in a preheated 350-degree oven for about 10 minutes, turning nuts after 5 minutes. Do not burn.

4. In the large bowl of an electric mixer fitted with a paddle or beaters, on medium speed soften the butter. Add the pistachio mixture, turn the speed to high, and beat until light and fluffy, stopping the mixer and scraping down the sides of the bowl and under the beaters as necessary, using a rubber spatula. Lower the speed to medium, add the eggs, one at a time, and the vanilla and almond extracts, and beat just to combine. Lower the speed, gradually pour in the flour, and mix just until combined.

5. Scrape the filling into the prepared tart shell and arrange the pieces of chocolate evenly around the top of the tart. Bake until the top is firm when lightly touched, 35 to 40 minutes. Cool on a rack. When completely cool, refrigerate, removing from the refrigerator 30 minutes before needed.

6. To serve, sift confectioners' sugar over the top of the tart. With a sharp knife, cut into slices and place each slice on a dessert plate. Garnish with a few fresh berries and, if desired, a small scoop of chocolate ice cream.

TO PREPARE AHEAD: Through step 5, the tart should be made early in the day and decorated just before serving.

CHOCOLATE-CHIP CHEESECAKE WITH CHERRY COMPOTE

Serves 8 to 10

This is by far the best-loved cheesecake at Spago Las Vegas. The combination of the cream and ricotta cheeses plus the addition of homemade chocolate chips gives this its very special flavor. When cherries are not in season, serve with Strawberry Compote (see page 216).

EQUIPMENT: 9-inch springform pan, small heatproof bowl, 11 × 15-inch baking tray, offset spatula, large heavy spatula or dough scraper, electric mixer with large bowl, rubber spatula, small nonreactive saucepan

6 OUNCES BITTERSWEET CHOCOLATE, CUT INTO SMALL PIECES	¾ TEASPOON SALT
	3 EGGS
CAKE	**CHERRY COMPOTE**
1½ POUNDS CREAM CHEESE, AT ROOM TEMPERATURE, CUT INTO 2-INCH PIECES	1 POUND FRESH CHERRIES, STEMMED
1¼ CUPS GRANULATED SUGAR	1 CUP GRANULATED SUGAR
8 OUNCES RICOTTA CHEESE	1 VANILLA BEAN, SPLIT LENGTHWISE AND SCRAPED
1 TEASPOON VANILLA EXTRACT	1 SMALL OR ½ LARGE CINNAMON STICK

1. Position the rack in the center of the oven and preheat the oven to 350 degrees. Lightly butter or coat with vegetable spray the bottom and sides of a 9-inch spring-form pan. Wrap heavy-duty foil (or two layers of regular foil) around the bottom and halfway up the outside of the pan, pleating to tighten. Set aside.

2. Make the chocolate chips: In a small heatproof bowl set over a pan of simmering water, melt the chocolate. When it is almost melted, remove from the heat, stir, and let it melt completely. Heat an 11 × 15-inch baking tray in the preheated oven for about 2 minutes. Invert the pan on a heatproof surface and spread the melted chocolate over the back of the pan. Spread, leveling with an offset spatula, first across the length and then the width of the pan. Refrigerate for 10 to 12 minutes.

3. Remove from the refrigerator and score the slightly hardened chocolate with the point of a small sharp knife. (To test whether the chocolate is firm enough, run the point of the knife across one way and then the other, making a few squares, about ½ inch wide. If the lines don't come together, the chocolate is ready to be scored. If

not, return to the refrigerator 1 or 2 minutes longer.) Run the knife down the length of the chocolate, making lines about $1/2$ inch apart (they do not have to be exact), then run the knife across the width of the pan, making tiny squares (again, no need for this to be exact). Return to the refrigerator to harden completely.

4. To remove the chocolate chips, using a large heavy spatula or dough scraper, scrape the chips off into a bowl. Set aside in a cool spot until needed.

5. Make the cake: In the large bowl of an electric mixer fitted with a paddle or beaters, on medium speed beat the cream cheese and sugar until smooth, stopping often to scrape down the sides of the bowl and under the beaters with a rubber spatula. Add the ricotta cheese, vanilla, and salt, and beat until well blended. Add the eggs and beat just until combined. Remove the bowl from the mixer and fold in the chocolate chips. Scrape into the prepared pan and set the pan in the center of a larger baking pan with sides. Pour enough hot water into the larger pan to reach about halfway up the sides of the springform pan, but not above the foil.

6. Carefully place both pans in the oven and bake until the cake is slightly firm in the center, about 1 hour and 15 minutes. (The cake will become firmer as it cools.) Remove the pans from the oven and *carefully* lift out the springform pan and place on a rack. Fold the foil down the sides of the pan to help cool the cake. When the cake has cooled, remove the foil and allow the cake to cool completely. Refrigerate, covered, overnight. (The cake should not be served until very firm.)

7. Meanwhile, make the Cherry Compote: With a cherry pitter or using a small knife, slightly slit each cherry and remove the pit, keeping the cherries whole. In a small nonreactive saucepan, combine the Cherry Compote ingredients and cook over medium heat until the cherries are tender, but still remain whole, about 15 minutes. Stir occasionally. (The natural juices from the cherries will come out and then start to thicken.) Let cool and then refrigerate, covered, in a small bowl.

8. When ready to serve, remove the cake from the refrigerator. Dip a long sharp knife into warm water and run the knife around the inside of the springform pan, loosening the cake from the pan. Remove the outer ring. To cut into slices, dip the knife into warm water as necessary. Place a slice of cheesecake in the center of a dessert plate and spoon a little of the Cherry Compote over.

TO PREPARE AHEAD: Through step 6, the cake must be made 1 day ahead. The compote can be prepared up to 2 days ahead.

CHOCOLATE CHEESECAKE

Serves 10 to 12

This is our favorite cheesecake. As with all our cheesecakes, it must be prepared a day early so that it is completely firm when served.

EQUIPMENT: 9-inch springform pan, rolling pin, small heatproof bowl, electric mixer with large bowl, rubber spatula, coarse strainer, baking pan with sides

¾ **POUND CHOCOLATE PÂTE SUCRÉE**	**8 OUNCES RICOTTA CHEESE**
(SEE PAGE 72)	½ **CUP SOUR CREAM**
6 OUNCES BITTERSWEET CHOCOLATE, CUT	**1 CUP SUGAR**
INTO SMALL PIECES	½ **TEASPOON VANILLA EXTRACT**
1½ **POUNDS CREAM CHEESE, AT ROOM**	½ **TEASPOON SALT**
TEMPERATURE, CUT INTO 2-INCH PIECES	**6 EGGS**

1. Position the rack in the center of the oven and preheat the oven to 350 degrees. Lightly butter or coat with vegetable spray the bottom and sides of a 9-inch spring-form pan.

2. Make the shell: On a lightly floured surface, roll out the Chocolate Pâte Sucrée to a circle a little larger than the 9-inch springform pan. Remove the bottom of the pan and, using the bottom as a guide, cut a 9-inch circle out of the dough. Roll the circle over the rolling pin and place the circle on the pan, trimming as necessary to fit. Bake 15 minutes, turning the pan after 8 minutes so that the crust will bake evenly. Cool on a rack and then fit the bottom back into the springform pan. Wrap heavy-duty aluminum foil (or two layers of regular foil) around the bottom and halfway up the outside of the pan, pleating to tighten. Set aside.

3. Make the cake: In a small heatproof bowl set over a pan of simmering water, melt the chocolate. When it is almost melted, remove from the heat, stir, and let melt completely. Keep warm.

4. Meanwhile, in the large bowl of an electric mixer fitted with a paddle or beaters, on medium speed beat the cream cheese, ricotta cheese, and sour cream until fluffy, stopping often to scrape down the sides and under the beaters with a rubber spatula. Add the sugar, vanilla, and salt, and beat until smooth. Add the eggs, one at a time, beating just until each egg is incorporated. Scrape in the melted chocolate and continue to beat until combined.

5. Strain through a coarse strainer and pour into the prepared pan, tapping once or twice on a firm surface to level. Set the pan in the center of a slightly larger baking pan with sides. Pour enough hot water into the larger pan to reach halfway up the sides of the springform pan, but not above the foil.

6. Carefully place both pans in the oven and bake until the top is slightly firm to the touch, 1 hour 10 minutes. (Cake will become firm as it cools.) Remove the pans from the oven, carefully lift out the springform pan, and place it on a rack. Fold the foil down the sides of the pan to help cool the cake. When the cake has cooled, remove the foil and allow the cake to cool completely. Refrigerate, covered with a clean piece of foil, overnight.

7. To serve, dip a long, sharp knife into warm water and run the knife around the inside of the springform pan, loosening the cake from the pan. Remove the outer ring. To cut into slices, dip the knife into warm water as necessary. Serve with Strawberry or Raspberry Compote (see page 216).

TO PREPARE AHEAD: Through step 6, the cake must be made 1 day but no more than 2 days ahead.

"COOKIES AND CREAM" CHEESECAKE

Serves 8 to 10

The chocolate crumble is used not only as a crust, but also as a layer and a topping. The result is a creamy cheesecake with a crunchy texture.

I find the easiest way to melt the white chocolate is to break it up into small pieces and place it in a small cup or bowl. Place the cup in the microwave oven, cover with a paper towel, and heat the chocolate, 30 seconds at a time, stopping the oven and stirring the chocolate, continuing to heat until melted. It shouldn't take more than two or three 30-second periods.

EQUIPMENT: 9- or 10-inch springform pan, baking tray, sifter, food processor, small cup or bowl, whisk, electric mixer with large bowl, rubber spatula, baking pan with sides

CHOCOLATE CRUMBLE	CAKE
1½ CUPS ALL-PURPOSE FLOUR	1½ POUNDS CREAM CHEESE, AT ROOM
1 CUP UNSWEETENED COCOA POWDER	TEMPERATURE, CUT INTO 2-INCH PIECES
1 CUP GRANULATED SUGAR	1 CUP GRANULATED SUGAR
¼ TEASPOON SALT	¼ TEASPOON SALT
4 OUNCES (1 STICK) UNSALTED BUTTER,	¾ CUP SOUR CREAM
CHILLED AND CUT INTO 1-OUNCE	3 EGGS
PIECES	2 TEASPOONS VANILLA EXTRACT
2 EGG YOLKS	4 OUNCES WHITE CHOCOLATE, MELTED
3 TABLESPOONS HEAVY CREAM	(SEE ABOVE)

1. Position the rack in the center of the oven and preheat the oven to 350 degrees. Butter or coat with vegetable spray the bottom of a 9- or 10-inch springform pan. Line a baking tray with parchment paper. Set aside.

2. Make the crumble: Sift together the flour, cocoa, sugar, and salt, and transfer to the workbowl of a food processor fitted with a steel blade. Process with on/off turns until blended. Arrange the pieces of butter around the flour mixture and process until the mixture resembles coarse meal.

3. In a small cup or bowl, whisk together the egg yolks and cream. With the processor running, pour the mixture through the feed tube, making certain you scrape out all the liquid from the cup. Let the machine run until the dough begins to come together, about 1 minute. (You should have about 4 cups.)

4. To make the crust, spoon 2 cups of the crumble into the prepared pan and press evenly over the bottom of the pan. (The rounded bottom of a 1-cup measuring cup is perfect for leveling the crust, ensuring smooth edges.)

5. Spread the remaining crumble on the prepared baking tray. Place the springform pan and baking tray in the oven and bake until the crumble is lightly toasted, 10 to 12 minutes. Transfer to a rack to cool. When completely cool, wrap heavy-duty aluminum foil, or two layers of regular foil, around the bottom and halfway up the outside of the springform pan, pleating the foil to tighten. Break up the crumble on the parchment paper, using your hands or a fork, and set aside.

6. Make the cake: Place the cheese, sugar, and salt in the large bowl of an electric mixer fitted with a paddle or beaters. On medium speed, beat until smooth, stopping often to scrape down the sides of the bowl and under the blade with a rubber spatula. Turn the speed to high and continue to beat until nice and creamy. Stop the mixer and add the sour cream, eggs, and vanilla, beat 3 minutes longer, again stopping the mixer and scraping down the sides of bowl and under the blade as necessary. Scrape in the melted chocolate and continue to beat until well combined and smooth. You should have about 6 cups of the mixture.

7. Pour half the mixture (3 cups) into the springform pan. Sprinkle half the crumble (1 cup) over, pour in the remaining 3 cups of the mixture and cover the entire surface with the remaining 1 cup of the crumble.

8. Set the springform pan in the center of a slightly larger baking pan with sides. Pour enough hot water into the larger pan to reach halfway up the sides of the springform pan, but not above the foil. Carefully place both pans in the oven and bake for 1 hour. Cover the cake loosely with foil and continue to bake until the center of the cake is slightly firm, 20 minutes longer. (Check the water level after 30 minutes, making certain there is enough water in the pan.)

9. Carefully remove both pans from the oven and transfer the springform pan to a rack to cool. Fold the foil down the sides of the pan, helping the cake to cool. When the cake has cooled remove the foil and allow the cake to cool completely. Cover the pan loosely with a clean piece of foil and refrigerate overnight.

10. When ready to serve, remove the cheesecake from the refrigerator. Dip a long sharp knife in warm water and run the knife around the inside of the springform pan, loosening the cake from the pan. Remove the outer ring. Continue to dip the knife into warm water as necessary for neatly cut slices.

11. To serve, arrange a slice of cake on a pretty cake plate and garnish with fresh berries of your choice, raspberries, blueberries, or sliced strawberries.

TO PREPARE AHEAD: The crust can be made 2 days ahead; the cake must be made 1 day ahead.

COOKIES AND CANDIES

*I*n every family there is a cookie monster lurking somewhere in the house, searching and sniffing for the sweet smell of cookie dough baking in the oven. In Mary's family, it's Michael; in Judy's family, well . . . it's Judy.

Cookies require the same attention to fine details that go into the preparation of perfect dough. You must use high-quality ingredients, measure carefully, and have good equipment. In many of our recipes we suggest rolling the cookie dough into small balls. A major advantage to this is that you can freeze the balls, remove as many as you need, pop them in the oven, and have freshly baked cookies at any given time—day or night.

Candy making is something that Mary became interested in a few years ago. Elegant homemade chocolates can be passed at the end of a meal and even your most finicky guests will find room for one, two . . . or more.

. . .

OATMEAL–CHOCOLATE CHUNK COOKIES

Makes about 5½ dozen cookies

These cookies are rich and chewy, with chunks of chocolate. We use bittersweet chocolate, but you can substitute milk or white chocolate. Just be sure that you use quick-cooking oats (which have been crushed further to speed up the cooking process). The cookies keep best in an airtight container or cookie jar.

EQUIPMENT: sifter, electric mixer with large bowl, 1 or 2 baking trays, wide metal spatula

1½ CUPS ALL-PURPOSE FLOUR

1 TEASPOON BAKING SODA

1 TEASPOON SALT

8 OUNCES (2 STICKS) UNSALTED BUTTER, AT ROOM TEMPERATURE, CUT INTO SMALL PIECES

1 CUP DARK BROWN SUGAR, FIRMLY PACKED

1 CUP GRANULATED SUGAR

2 EGGS

1 TEASPOON VANILLA EXTRACT

1 POUND COARSELY CHOPPED BITTERSWEET CHOCOLATE (PIECES ABOUT THE SIZE OF LARGE CHOCOLATE CHIPS)

2 CUPS QUICK-COOKING OATS

1½ CUPS (ABOUT 5 OUNCES), PECANS, TOASTED AND CHOPPED (SEE FOOTNOTE FOR TOASTING HAZELNUTS, PAGE 21)

1. Sift together the flour, baking soda, and salt. Set aside.

2. In the large bowl of an electric mixer fitted with a paddle or beaters, on medium speed soften the butter. Add the brown and granulated sugars, raising the speed to high when the sugar is incorporated, and continue to mix until fluffy, scraping down the sides of the bowl and under the beaters as necessary. Lower the speed to medium and add the eggs, one at a time, and the vanilla, again scraping down the sides of the bowl as necessary. Turn the speed to low, gradually pour in the flour mixture, and beat just until combined. Stop the machine. Add the chocolate, oats, and pecans, and again beat just until combined.

3. Scrape the dough out of the bowl and wrap in plastic wrap. Refrigerate until firm, 2 to 3 hours.

4. Position the rack in the center of the oven and preheat the oven to 350 degrees. Line one or two baking trays with parchment paper.

5. Remove the dough from the refrigerator and divide it into mounds, about 1 ounce each (about the size of an unshelled walnut). Roll between the palms of your hands, forming about 65 cookies. Arrange the balls on the prepared trays about 2 inches apart. Bake until slightly firm to the touch, 13 to 15 minutes, reversing the trays back to front after 7 minutes to ensure even baking. Place the trays on racks to cool. After a few minutes, remove the cookies with a wide metal spatula and transfer to the rack to cool completely. If reusing the baking tray, cool slightly before arranging balls of dough on it.

TO PREPARE AHEAD: In step 5, the balls of dough can be rolled, placed on trays, wrapped well in plastic wrap, and refrigerated until needed, up to 1 week. They can be frozen for up to 2 months.

CHOCOLATE THUMBPRINT COOKIES

All kids have a natural instinct for sticking their fingers into everything, so they will have great fun helping you make these cookies.

EQUIPMENT: 1 or 2 baking trays, sifter, small heatproof bowl, electric mixer with large bowl, rubber spatula

3 CUPS PLUS 3 TABLESPOONS ALL-PURPOSE FLOUR	¾ POUND (3 STICKS) UNSALTED BUTTER, AT ROOM TEMPERATURE, CUT INTO SMALL PIECES
¼ CUP UNSWEETENED COCOA POWDER	1⅓ CUPS CONFECTIONERS' SUGAR, SIFTED
¼ TEASPOON SALT	2 EGG YOLKS
4 OUNCES BITTERSWEET CHOCOLATE, CUT INTO SMALL PIECES	RASPBERRY JAM OR GANACHE (SEE PAGE 209)

1. Line one or two baking trays with parchment paper and set aside.

2. Sift together the flour, cocoa, and salt. Set aside.

3. In a small heatproof bowl set over a pan of simmering water, melt the chocolate. When almost melted, turn off the heat and allow it to melt completely, stirring occasionally.

4. In the large bowl of an electric mixer fitted with a paddle or beaters, beat the butter and confectioners' sugar. Start on low speed until the sugar is incorporated into the butter, then turn the speed to high and continue to beat until the mixture is very fluffy and white, about 5 minutes, scraping down the sides of the bowl and under the beaters with a rubber spatula as necessary.

5. On medium speed, add the egg yolks, one at a time, beating just to combine after each addition. Add the melted chocolate and mix well. On low speed, slowly pour in the sifted ingredients, again beating just until incorporated into the dough. Do not overmix.

6. Remove the bowl from the mixer and form small balls of dough, about $1/2$ ounce each. Gently press your thumb into each ball, making a deep indentation in the center of the ball of dough, and then place the balls on the prepared baking tray. Refrigerate for 1 to 2 hours, up to overnight. This will help keep the indentation in the dough.

7. Position the rack in the center of the oven and preheat the oven to 350 degrees.

8. Arrange the balls, about 2 inches apart, on the prepared baking trays. (If using only one baking tray, cool between uses, before arranging more dough on the tray.) Bake about 12 minutes, turning tray(s) back to front after 6 minutes. Cool on a rack. When completely cool, fill the indentation with a little raspberry jam or Ganache.

TO PREPARE AHEAD: Through step 8, the cookies can be prepared and stored in an airtight container. Fill the indentation just before serving.

FROSTED CHOCOLATE SHORTBREAD COOKIES

Makes about 4 dozen cookies

These are pretty addictive. No one can eat just one, so make sure to bake enough. If you like, 1 tablespoon of instant espresso can be sifted along with the flour, cocoa, cinnamon, and salt.

EQUIPMENT: sifter, electric mixer with large bowl, rubber spatula, 1 or 2 baking trays, pastry bag with #3 plain tip, small metal spatula

1⅓ **CUPS ALL-PURPOSE FLOUR**	1 **CUP GRANULATED SUGAR**
¾ **CUP UNSWEETENED COCOA POWDER**	1 **EGG**
¾ **TEASPOON GROUND CINNAMON**	1½ **TEASPOONS VANILLA EXTRACT**
⅛ **TEASPOON SALT**	½ **RECIPE CHOCOLATE MOUSSE**
6 **OUNCES** (1½ **STICKS**) **UNSALTED BUTTER,**	**(SEE PAGE 195)**
AT ROOM TEMPERATURE, CUT INTO	**WHITE CHOCOLATE CURLS (SEE PAGE 213)**
SMALL PIECES	

1. Make the cookies: Sift together the flour, cocoa, cinnamon, and salt. Set aside.

2. In the large bowl of an electric mixer fitted with a paddle or beaters, on medium speed soften the butter. Add the sugar, and when incorporated, raise the speed to high, and continue to mix until fluffy, scraping down the sides of the bowl and under the beaters with a rubber spatula as necessary. Lower the speed to medium, add the egg and vanilla, and beat just to combine. Stop the machine, add the flour mixture, and on low speed mix until just combined.

3. Scrape the dough out of the bowl and onto a flat work surface. (If too soft, wrap in plastic wrap and refrigerate until slightly firm, about 1 hour.) With lightly floured hands, form a somewhat flat log about 12 inches long and 1½ inches wide. Wrap in plastic wrap, place on a baking tray, and refrigerate until very firm, at least 3 hours, up to overnight.

4. Position the rack in the center of the oven and preheat the oven to 350 degrees. Line one or two baking trays with parchment paper.

5. Remove the dough from the refrigerator and unwrap. Using a very sharp knife, cut the log into thin slices, about ¼ inch each. Arrange on the prepared baking tray(s) about 1 inch apart, and bake for 10 minutes, turning the tray(s) back to front after 5 minutes. Cool on a rack.

6. When cool, remove from the tray and frost with the Chocolate Mousse: Fit a pastry bag with a #3 plain tip and fill with the mousse. Pipe a thin layer over the top of each cookie and smooth with a small metal spatula. Refrigerate until firm. When firm, garnish with the White Chocolate Curls and again refrigerate until needed.

7. To serve, arrange on a doily-lined tray and allow guests to help themselves.

TO PREPARE AHEAD: Through step 5, cookies can be prepared 1 day ahead. Frost before serving. Baked cookies can be stored in an airtight container.

CHOCOLATE CHUNK COOKIES

Makes 50 to 52 cookies

The name says it all!

EQUIPMENT: sifter, electric mixer with large bowl, 1 or 2 baking trays, rubber spatula, wide metal spatula

1 ½ CUPS ALL-PURPOSE FLOUR	½ CUP GRANULATED SUGAR
1 TEASPOON BAKING SODA	2 EGGS
1 TEASPOON SALT	2 TEASPOONS VANILLA EXTRACT
8 OUNCES (2 STICKS) UNSALTED BUTTER, AT ROOM TEMPERATURE, CUT INTO SMALL PIECES	12 OUNCES COARSELY CHOPPED SEMISWEET CHOCOLATE (PIECES ABOUT THE SIZE OF LARGE CHOCOLATE CHIPS)
1 CUP LIGHT BROWN SUGAR, FIRMLY PACKED	6 OUNCES UNSALTED CASHEWS, TOASTED,* COOLED, AND COARSELY CHOPPED

1. Sift together the flour, baking soda, and salt. Set aside.

2. In the large bowl of an electric mixer fitted with a paddle or beaters, on medium speed soften the butter. Add the brown and granulated sugars. When the sugar is incorporated, raise the speed to high and continue to mix until fluffy, stopping the machine and scraping down the sides of the bowl and under the beaters with a rubber spatula as necessary.

3. Lower the speed to medium and add the eggs, one at a time, beating just to combine, and the vanilla. Stop the machine and add the flour mixture. On low speed, beat just until incorporated. Add the chocolate and nuts, and beat just until combined. Scrape the dough out of the bowl and wrap in plastic wrap. Refrigerate until slightly firm, about 1 hour.

4. Position the rack in the center of the oven and preheat the oven to 350 degrees. Line one or two baking trays with parchment paper.

5. Remove the dough from the refrigerator and divide into mounds, about 1 ounce each (the size of an unshelled walnut). Roll between the palms of your hands, forming 50

* To toast the cashews, arrange the nuts on a baking tray in one layer. Bake in a 350-degree oven for 10 to 12 minutes, turning occasionally and watching carefully to prevent burning.

to 52 small balls. Arrange the balls on the prepared trays about 2 inches apart. Bake until just firm to the touch, 14 to 15 minutes, reversing the trays from front to back after 7 or 8 minutes. Place the trays on racks and when slightly cool, after about 5 minutes, remove the cookies from the trays with a wide metal spatula to cool completely on the racks. If reusing the baking tray, cool slightly before arranging more balls of dough on it.

TO PREPARE AHEAD: In step 5, balls of dough can be rolled, placed on the tray, and refrigerated until ready to bake. You can bake a few or all as needed. Baked cookies can be stored in an airtight container.

MOCHA–MACADAMIA NUT–CHOCOLATE CHUNK COOKIES

Makes about 5 dozen cookies

The macadamia nut is a gourmet's delight. When combined with chocolate it becomes a most welcome taste experience.

EQUIPMENT: sifter, electric mixer with large bowl, rubber spatula, 1 or 2 baking trays, wide metal spatula

2¼ CUPS ALL-PURPOSE FLOUR

¼ CUP UNSWEETENED COCOA POWDER

1½ TEASPOONS INSTANT ESPRESSO

1 TEASPOON BAKING SODA

½ TEASPOON SALT

8 OUNCES (2 STICKS) UNSALTED BUTTER, AT ROOM TEMPERATURE, CUT INTO SMALL PIECES

¾ CUP DARK BROWN SUGAR, FIRMLY PACKED

¾ CUP GRANULATED SUGAR

2 EGGS

2 TEASPOONS VANILLA EXTRACT

8 OUNCES COARSELY CHOPPED BITTERSWEET CHOCOLATE (PIECES ABOUT THE SIZE OF LARGE CHOCOLATE CHIPS)

1½ CUPS UNSALTED MACADAMIA NUTS, COARSELY CHOPPED

1. Sift together the flour, cocoa, espresso, baking soda, and salt. Set aside.

2. In the large bowl of an electric mixer fitted with a paddle or beaters, on medium speed soften the butter. Add the brown and granulated sugars. When the sugar is incorporated, raise the speed to high and continue to beat until fluffy, scraping down the sides of the bowl and under the beaters with a rubber spatula as necessary. Lower the speed to medium and add the eggs, one at a time, and the vanilla, again scraping the sides of the bowl as necessary. Turn the speed to low, gradually pour in the flour mixture, and beat just until combined. Add the chocolate and nuts and again beat just until combined.

3. Scrape the dough out of the bowl and wrap in plastic wrap. Refrigerate 2 or 3 hours, up to overnight.

4. Position the rack in the center of the oven and preheat the oven to 350 degrees. Line one or two baking trays with parchment paper.

5. Remove the dough from the refrigerator and divide into mounds, about 1 ounce each (the size of an unshelled walnut). Roll between the palms of your hands, forming 60 to 62 balls of dough. Arrange the balls on the prepared trays about 2 inches apart. Bake until slightly firm to the touch, 13 to 15 minutes, reversing the trays front to back after 7 minutes to ensure even baking. Place the trays on racks to cool. After a few minutes transfer the cookies to the racks with a wide metal spatula to continue to cool. If reusing the baking tray, cool slightly before arranging balls of dough on it.

TO PREPARE AHEAD: In step 5, balls of dough can be rolled, placed on the tray, and refrigerated until ready to bake. Baked cookies can be stored in an airtight container.

PEANUT BUTTER-CHOCOLATE CHUNK COOKIES

Makes about 5 dozen cookies

What a combination! This cookie dough is so delicious Mary has to hide the batter. The cooks love it even before it's baked.

EQUIPMENT: sifter, electric mixer with large bowl, rubber spatula, 1 or 2 baking trays, wide metal spatula

2¼ CUPS ALL-PURPOSE FLOUR	⅔ CUP CREAMY PEANUT BUTTER
1 TEASPOON BAKING SODA	2 EGGS
1 TEASPOON SALT	2 TEASPOONS VANILLA EXTRACT
8 OUNCES (2 STICKS) UNSALTED BUTTER,	1 POUND MILK CHOCOLATE, COARSELY
AT ROOM TEMPERATURE, CUT INTO	CHOPPED (PIECES ABOUT THE SIZE OF
SMALL PIECES	LARGE CHOCOLATE CHIPS)
2 CUPS DARK BROWN SUGAR, FIRMLY	1½ CUPS UNSALTED PEANUTS, TOASTED,*
PACKED	COOLED, AND COARSELY CHOPPED

1. Sift together the flour, baking soda, and salt. Set aside.

2. In the large bowl of an electric mixer fitted with a paddle or beaters, on medium speed soften the butter. Add the sugar, raise the speed to high, and beat until fluffy, scraping down the sides of the bowl and under the beaters with a rubber spatula as necessary. Add the peanut butter and beat until incorporated. Lower the speed and add the eggs, one at a time, and the vanilla, again scraping down the sides of the bowl as necessary. Turn the speed to low, gradually pour in the flour mixture, and beat just until combined. Add the chocolate and peanuts, and again beat just until combined.

3. Scrape the dough out of the bowl, wrap in plastic wrap, and refrigerate until firm, 2 to 3 hours.

4. Position the rack in the center of the oven and preheat the oven to 350 degrees. Line one or two baking trays with parchment paper.

---

* To toast the peanuts, arrange them on a baking tray in a single layer. Place in a 350-degree oven and bake about 8 minutes, turning the nuts after 3 or 4 minutes, being careful that they do not burn. You want them to be slightly toasted, not browned.

5. Remove the dough from the refrigerator and divide into mounds, about 1 ounce each (about the size of an unshelled walnut). Roll between the palms of your hands, forming about 60 cookies. Arrange the balls on the prepared trays about 2 inches apart. Bake until slightly firm to the touch, 14 to 15 minutes, reversing trays back to front after 7 minutes to ensure even baking. Place the trays on racks to cool and after a few minutes, remove the cookies with a wide metal spatula and place on the racks to continue to cool. If reusing the tray, let it cool before arranging balls of dough on it.

TO PREPARE AHEAD: In step 5, balls of dough can be rolled, placed on the tray, and refrigerated until needed. Baked cookies can be stored in an airtight container.

HOLIDAY PINWHEEL COOKIES

Makes 5½ to 6 dozen cookies

This is a fun cookie to make. The beautiful pinwheel effect is achieved by sandwiching two different doughs and rolling them together into a log before slicing. These make delectable holiday gifts.

EQUIPMENT: sifter, electric mixer with large bowl, rubber spatula, rolling pin, 1 or 2 baking trays, 12 × 16 inches

3 CUPS ALL-PURPOSE FLOUR

1 TEASPOON BAKING POWDER

½ TEASPOON SALT

6 OUNCES (1½ STICKS) UNSALTED BUTTER, AT ROOM TEMPERATURE, CUT INTO SMALL PIECES

1½ CUPS GRANULATED SUGAR

1 VANILLA BEAN, SPLIT LENGTHWISE AND SCRAPED*

2 EGG YOLKS

⅓ CUP MILK

4 OUNCES BITTERSWEET CHOCOLATE, MELTED AND KEPT SLIGHTLY WARM

1 TEASPOON FINELY CHOPPED OR GRATED ORANGE RIND

1 EGG WHITE, LIGHTLY BEATEN

1. Sift together the flour, baking powder, and salt. Set aside.

2. In the large bowl of an electric mixer fitted with a paddle or beaters, on medium speed soften the butter. Lower the speed and gradually add the sugar, then the scrapings from the vanilla bean. Turn the speed to high and beat until fluffy, scraping down the sides of the bowl and under the beaters with a rubber spatula as necessary.

3. Add the egg yolks, one at a time, beating just to combine after each addition. Turn the speed to low and alternate adding the flour mixture and milk, starting and ending with the flour mixture (three additions of flour and two of milk).

4. Divide the dough into two parts. The larger should be 1 pound 4 ounces, the smaller one, 1 pound. Wrap the larger piece of dough in plastic wrap and return the smaller one to the mixing bowl. Scrape the melted chocolate into the bowl, add the orange rind, and mix until well incorporated (the chocolate dough will now weigh 1 pound

*If a vanilla bean is not available, add 1 teaspoon vanilla extract with the egg yolks.

4 ounces). Wrap each piece of dough in plastic wrap, flatten, and refrigerate until just firm, 2 to 3 hours. (If it's too firm to roll when taken out of the refrigerator, let it rest 15 to 20 minutes, then roll.)

5. Place a large sheet of parchment or wax paper (at least 10 × 16 inches) on a firm surface. Sprinkle lightly with flour, place the plain dough on the paper, and roll out to a rectangle, about 9 × 14 inches, lightly flouring the dough as necessary. Brush away any excess flour. Carefully pick up the paper with the rolled-out dough and place it on the back of a baking tray (about 12 × 16 inches) and set the tray in the refrigerator while rolling out the remaining piece of dough.

6. Place another sheet of parchment paper on a firm surface, sprinkle lightly with flour, and roll out the chocolate dough to the same size rectangle as the plain dough (9 × 14 inches). If the chocolate dough is too soft, refrigerate it for a few minutes. Remove the baking tray with the plain dough from the refrigerator and brush with beaten egg white. Carefully invert the paper with the chocolate dough atop the plain dough and then gently peel away the paper. If the chocolate dough comes apart as you do this, just piece it together. Use your fingers or a rolling pin to match up the edges. With the 14-inch side in front of you and the bottom sheet of paper to aid you, roll up the dough lengthwise into a long roll, using the paper as a guide, enclosing the chocolate layer within the plain layer. Be careful that you do not roll the paper into the dough. Straighten the roll to about a 19-inch length (2 inches in diameter) and place it on a large tray or on a flat shelf of the refrigerator. Refrigerate until very firm, 4 hours, up to overnight.

7. Position the rack in the center of the oven and preheat the oven to 350 degrees. Line one or two baking trays with parchment paper.

8. Remove the roll of dough from the refrigerator, unwrap and place it on a firm surface. Trim each end of the roll (to be baked and eaten by the family). Cut the roll into slices, between ¼ and ⅓ inch wide, and arrange on prepared trays, about 2 inches apart. Bake until lightly golden, 15 to 17 minutes, turning the trays back to front after 7 or 8 minutes. Cool on a rack.

TO PREPARE AHEAD: Through step 6, the dough can be refrigerated overnight. Baked cookies can be stored in an airtight container.

CHOCOLATE TRUFFLE SANDWICH COOKIES

Makes 20 cookies

These are particularly delicate and delicious. The Ganache sandwiched between the two cookies is the perfect filling, fudgy but not too sweet. We suggest a thin layer of Ganache, but if you prefer a thicker filling, adjust it to your taste and increase the amount of Ganache. If you want to serve this as an end-of-the-meal dessert, set one of the cookies on a large dessert plate, pipe a generous amount of Ganache over the cookie, top with a second cookie, a second layer of Ganache, then a third cookie. Melted white chocolate drizzled over the last cookie is the finishing touch. Surround with fresh raspberries and sift confectioners' sugar around the plate.

EQUIPMENT: 1 or 2 baking trays, rolling pin, 2¼-inch cookie cutter, small heatproof bowl, wide-tined fork or truffle fork

CHOCOLATE PÂTE SUCRÉE (SEE PAGE 72)
ABOUT 1 CUP GANACHE (SEE PAGE 209)

3 OUNCES WHITE CHOCOLATE, CUT INTO SMALL PIECES

1. Position the rack in the center of the oven and preheat the oven to 350 degrees. Line one or two baking trays with parchment paper. Set aside.

2. Make the cookies: Follow the recipe for Chocolate Pâte Sucrée. On a lightly floured surface, roll the dough out to a rectangle, about 12 × 20 inches. Using a 2¼-inch cookie cutter,* cut out 28 circles. Reroll the scraps of dough and roll into a 12 × 10-inch rectangle. Cut out 12 more circles. As the circles are cut out, arrange them on the prepared trays. These cookies don't spread very much so they can be placed about 1 inch apart. Refrigerate for 30 to 40 minutes.

3. Remove the trays from the refrigerator and prick the circles with the tines of a fork, making a decorative pattern. (This will also keep them flat.) Bake 13 to 14 minutes, reversing the trays back to front after 7 minutes. Do not overbake. Cool on a rack.

4. When the Ganache is of spreading consistency, like the texture of creamy peanut butter, spread a thin layer (about 1 tablespoon) over one side of a cookie, the side not pricked with the fork. Cover with a second cookie, again the side with the deco-

---

* At the restaurant, we also cut out tiny cookies, layer with a dab of Ganache, and serve as part of a cookie assortment. It's just the right size to pop into your mouth.

ration on the outside. Repeat with the remaining cookies and Ganache. (If you have Ganache left over, it can be refrigerated, covered, for up to 3 weeks.)

5. In a small heatproof bowl set over a pan of simmering water, melt the white chocolate. Using a wide-tined fork or truffle fork, drizzle the chocolate over the top of each of the sandwich cookies.

TO PREPARE AHEAD: Through step 4 or 5, cookies will keep in an airtight container for up to 1 week.

CHOCOLATE-DIPPED GINGER BISCOTTI

Makes 5 to 5½ dozen cookies

The spiciness of the ginger complements the sweet taste of the chocolate. We chose to dip one end of the biscotti in white chocolate and the other end in bittersweet chocolate, but if you prefer, you can use one or the other. You can also dip only one end in the chocolate. We cut the biscotti on a sharp angle, ⅓ to ½ inch thick, 5 to 6 inches long. It can also be cut straight across, resulting in smaller biscotti and a larger number. These make excellent gifts; they are easy to prepare, they keep well, and one batch yields many cookies.

EQUIPMENT: sifter, electric mixer with large bowl, rubber spatula, 1 or 2 baking trays, rolling pin, 1 or 2 racks to fit into baking trays, long serrated knife, 2 small heat-proof bowls, small flat metal spatula, preferably an offset spatula

4 CUPS ALL-PURPOSE FLOUR

2 TABLESPOONS GROUND GINGER

1½ TEASPOONS BAKING POWDER

⅛ TEASPOON GROUND WHITE PEPPER

8 OUNCES (2 STICKS) UNSALTED BUTTER, AT ROOM TEMPERATURE, CUT INTO SMALL PIECES

1¾ CUPS GRANULATED SUGAR

4 EGGS

1½ TEASPOONS VANILLA EXTRACT

1 CUP (6 OUNCES) CRYSTALLIZED GINGER, COARSELY CHOPPED

1 EGG WHITE, LIGHTLY BEATEN, FOR EGG WASH

8 OUNCES BITTERSWEET CHOCOLATE, CUT INTO SMALL PIECES

8 OUNCES WHITE CHOCOLATE, CUT INTO SMALL PIECES

1. Make the cookies: Sift together the flour, ground ginger, baking powder, and pepper. Set aside.

2. In the large bowl of an electric mixer fitted with a paddle or beaters, beat the butter and sugar. Start on low speed until slightly blended, then raise the speed to high and continue to beat until fluffy, scraping down the sides of the bowl and under the beaters with a rubber spatula as necessary.

3. Turn the speed to medium and add the eggs, one at a time, beating just to combine after each addition, and the vanilla. Stop the machine. Add the sifted ingredients and the crystallized ginger, and beat on low speed just until incorporated into the dough.

4. Divide the dough into two equal portions, each about 1 pound, 9 ounces. On a lightly floured surface, with lightly floured hands, roll out each portion into a log, about 17 inches long and 2 inches in diameter. The dough will be sticky. For easier handling, we recommend laying a long piece of plastic wrap on a flat surface and sprinkling lightly with flour. Transfer the dough onto the plastic, enclosing and then rolling to the desired length. Wrap each log in plastic wrap, place on a flat baking tray, and refrigerate until firm, 2 to 3 hours.

5. Position the rack in the center of the oven and preheat the oven to 325 degrees. Line a baking tray with parchment paper.

6. When the dough is firm, unwrap the logs and place on the prepared baking tray, about 4 inches apart. The logs will spread during the baking process, so if the baking tray is not wide enough, use a second tray. Brush each log with egg wash and bake until golden, 35 to 40 minutes. (There will be cracks on the surface of the logs—that's okay. This is an indication that the logs have baked sufficiently.) Transfer the baking tray(s) to a rack and let the logs cool thoroughly. Do not remove the logs from the tray while warm; they are still soft and might break. When completely cool, wrap each log in plastic wrap, place it back on the baking tray, and refrigerate overnight.

7. When ready to finish baking the biscotti, preheat the oven to 275 degrees. Fit a rack into a baking tray.

8. Unwrap a log and place on a firm cutting board. Using a long serrated knife, with a sawing motion and on a sharp angle, cut off one of the ends. Continue to cut slices at a sharp angle, about $\frac{1}{4}$ to $\frac{1}{3}$ inch wide and 5 inches long, making about 30 to 35 slices. Arrange the slices on the rack in the baking tray (use the ends, too, for family consumption) and bake until the biscotti are lightly golden, 25 to 30 minutes, turning the baking tray back to front after 15 minutes. At first the biscotti will be soft, but as they bake they will harden. Remove the tray from the oven and let cool on a rack. Do not remove the biscotti until cool. Repeat with the remaining log.

9. Meanwhile, place the chocolates in separate small heatproof bowls and melt each over a pan of simmering water. Keep warm.

10. Dip the biscotti: Carefully dip one end of each biscotti into the melted chocolate, allowing excess chocolate to drip back into the bowl. If you find the chocolate coating too thick, scrape a little of the warm chocolate off with a small offset spatula. As each biscotti is coated with chocolate, place on a tray lined with parchment or wax paper until the chocolate hardens. (If coating with both dark and white chocolates, dip in the dark chocolate first, allow it to harden, and then coat the opposite end with the white chocolate.) Repeat with the remaining biscotti and chocolates. Store in an airtight container.

TO PREPARE AHEAD: Through step 4 or step 6, the logs can be wrapped well and frozen. Defrost, wrapped, in the refrigerator and continue with the recipe. Through step 10, biscotti will keep 2 to 3 weeks.

ORANGE-CHOCOLATE CHIP BISCOTTI

Makes about 5 dozen cookies

Biscotti can be sliced as described below, at a sharp angle, or straight across, making smaller slices. The number of slices depends on how the logs are sliced. Biscotti harden the longer they are stored. But they soften—and are even tastier—when dipped in wine, coffee, or milk. Adding the orange zest while creaming the butter maximizes its flavor.

EQUIPMENT: sifter, electric mixer with large bowl, rubber spatula, 1 or 2 baking trays, 1 or 2 racks to fit baking trays, long serrated knife

3 1/2 **CUPS ALL-PURPOSE FLOUR**	3 **EGGS**
3/4 **TABLESPOON BAKING POWDER**	1/4 **CUP ORANGE JUICE**
1/2 **TEASPOON SALT**	1 1/2 **TEASPOONS GRAND MARNIER**
6 **OUNCES (**1 1/2 **STICKS) UNSALTED BUTTER,**	8 **OUNCES SEMISWEET CHOCOLATE CHIPS**
AT ROOM TEMPERATURE, CUT INTO	**OR BITTERSWEET CHOCOLATE, CUT**
PIECES	**INTO VERY SMALL PIECES**
2/3 **CUP GRANULATED SUGAR**	1 **EGG WHITE, LIGHTLY BEATEN FOR EGG**
FINELY CHOPPED ZEST OF 2 LARGE	**WASH**
ORANGES	**ABOUT 2 TABLESPOONS CRYSTAL SUGAR**

1. Sift together the flour, baking powder, and salt. Set aside.

2. In the large bowl of an electric mixer fitted with a paddle or beaters, beat the butter, granulated sugar, and orange zest. Start on low speed until slightly blended, then raise the speed to high and continue to beat until fluffy, scraping down the sides of the bowl and under the beaters with a rubber spatula as necessary.

3. Turn the speed to medium and add the eggs, one at a time, beating just to combine after each addition. Add the orange juice and Grand Marnier. On low speed, slowly pour in the sifted ingredients and beat just until combined. Add the chocolate chips and again, beat just until combined. (The dough will be thick and cling to the beaters.)

4. With lightly floured hands, remove the dough from the bowl and divide into two equal portions, each about 1 pound 5 ounces. On a lightly floured surface, form

each portion into a log, about 15 inches long and 1 inch in diameter. Wrap each log in plastic wrap, place on a baking tray, and refrigerate until firm, about 3 hours.

5. Position the rack in the center of the oven and preheat the oven to 325 degrees. Line a baking tray with parchment paper.

6. When firm, unwrap one of the logs and place on the prepared baking tray. If placing two logs on one tray, make certain they are about 4 inches apart, because the logs will spread during the baking process. Brush each log with egg wash and sprinkle about 1 tablespoon crystal sugar down the length of the log. Bake until lightly colored and slightly firm to the touch, about 35 minutes. (There will be cracks on the tops of the logs. That's okay.) Place the tray on a rack and let the logs cool. Do not remove the log from the tray while hot; the log will be soft and might break. When *completely* cool, wrap in plastic wrap and carefully set it on a flat surface in the refrigerator (the bottom of the refrigerator or back on the baking tray) overnight. If the logs are placed directly on refrigerator racks, the ends might curl under, because the logs are still not completely firm.

7. The next day, preheat the oven to 275 degrees. Fit a rack into a baking tray.

8. Unwrap one of the logs and place it on a cutting board. With a long serrated knife, using a sawing motion, and on a sharp angle, cut off one of the ends. Carefully cut slices at a sharp angle, a scant ½ inch thick and about 4 inches long, making 28 to 30 slices. (Don't discard the ends. They are just as good to eat.) Arrange the slices on the rack in the baking tray and bake until the slices harden, 25 to 30 minutes. At first the slices will be soft, but they will harden as they bake. Repeat with the remaining log. Cool on the rack. Store in an airtight container.

TO PREPARE AHEAD: Through step 4 or 6, logs can be well wrapped and frozen. Defrost, wrapped, in the refrigerator, and continue with the recipe. Through step 8, biscotti will keep for 2 to 3 weeks.

CRUNCHY MINT-CHOCOLATE TRUFFLES

Makes 80 to 100 truffles

Judy's son Peter once described to Mary a very special, very delicious chocolate that he had eaten in England. The result is our Crunchy Mint-Chocolate Truffle, a very rich bon-bon that literally melts in your mouth. When cutting the chocolate into squares, do not try to measure each square; if you do, you'll find making these a tedious chore. Just cut the bar into strips as described below, measure the first few truffles, and then cut into small squares, using your eyes to judge the size. The truffles can be placed in tiny foil or paper cups and refrigerated or frozen.

EQUIPMENT: 2 medium heatproof bowls, 2 small saucepans, rubber spatula, 12 × 17 × 1-inch baking tray, candy thermometer, long-handled wooden spoon, small metal spatula, rolling pin, 9-inch square pan, propane torch, optional

TRUFFLE BASE
- 1 POUND BITTERSWEET OR SEMISWEET CHOCOLATE, CUT INTO VERY SMALL PIECES
- ¾ CUP HEAVY CREAM
- 2 TABLESPOONS PEPPERMINT OR MINT EXTRACT
- 3 OUNCES (¾ STICK) UNSALTED BUTTER, CUT INTO VERY SMALL PIECES

MINT CRUNCH
- ¾ CUP GRANULATED SUGAR
- 3 TABLESPOONS LIGHT CORN SYRUP
- 3 TABLESPOONS WATER
- 1 TABLESPOON MINT EXTRACT
- 4 OUNCES (1 STICK) UNSALTED BUTTER, CUT INTO SMALL PIECES
- ½ TEASPOON SALT

CHOCOLATE COATING
- 8 TO 10 OUNCES SEMISWEET OR MILK CHOCOLATE, CUT INTO SMALL PIECES

1. Make the truffle base: Place the small pieces of chocolate in a medium heatproof bowl and set aside. In a small saucepan, bring the cream and mint extract to a boil. Pour this mixture over the chocolate and gently stir with a rubber spatula until the chocolate is melted. Add the butter and let it melt into the chocolate mixture, stirring occasionally. Set aside to thicken.

2. Make the mint crunch: Coat a 12 × 17 × 1-inch baking tray with vegetable oil or vegetable spray and set aside. In a clean small saucepan, combine the sugar, corn syrup, water, and mint extract and, over medium heat, bring to a boil. Let boil until

large bubbles form on the surface, about 3 minutes. Cover with foil or a lid and boil 5 minutes longer.

3. Add the butter and continue cooking, uncovered, over medium heat, until the temperature reaches 300 degrees on a candy thermometer, 10 to 15 minutes. Make sure the thermometer does not touch the bottom of the pan when testing or the reading won't be accurate. Remove the pan from the heat and immediately add the salt, stirring with a long-handled wooden spoon.

4. Pour the mixture onto the oiled baking tray, and using a small metal spatula, spread out as much as possible, making a thin mint candy layer. Set aside to cool.

5. Arrange a few layers of paper towel on a clean board. Invert the cooled pan over the toweling, tapping the pan a few times to release the mint candy bar. Using the paper towel, dab away the excess oil. Break the bar into pieces, enclose in a plastic bag, and secure with a tie. Run a rolling pin over the plastic bag until you have tiny bits of mint candy. Stir the candy into the reserved truffle base and combine thoroughly.

6. Make the truffle block: Line a 9-inch square pan with plastic wrap or wax paper, the paper long enough to drape over two opposite sides of the pan. Spoon the chocolate mixture into the pan, spreading it out as evenly as possible. Refrigerate until firmly set, 1 to 2 hours.

7. Make the chocolate coating: In a medium heatproof bowl set over a pan of simmering water, melt the chocolate. When almost melted, turn off the heat and allow to melt completely, stirring occasionally.

8. Remove the truffle block from the refrigerator, invert it onto a clean cutting board, and peel away the wrapping. Using a long, very sharp knife, cut into ¾-inch squares. The easiest way to do this is to first cut the block into ¾-inch-long strips and then cut each strip into squares. If you have a propane torch, use it to heat the knife as needed before cutting. If not, run the knife under very hot water as necessary, dry the knife thoroughly, and then cut.

9. Coat the truffles with chocolate: Place two or three truffles into the melted chocolate. Remove by placing the tines of a fork under each truffle, allowing any excess chocolate to drip back into the bowl. Place the coated truffle on a tray lined with wax paper or plastic wrap to harden. As each truffle hardens, set into a small paper or foil cup, arrange on a tray, and refrigerate.

TO PREPARE AHEAD: Through step 6, the truffle block can be made 1 or 2 days before completing the recipe. Through step 9, the truffles can be refrigerated for up to 1 week and frozen for up to 3 months.

FLORIDA CHOCOLATE-DIPPED COCONUT PATTIES

When I was fourteen, my family moved to Florida from Massachusetts. During the drive down, my mother bought a box of coconut patties. We couldn't get enough of them. This recipe is fashioned after that sweet memory.

EQUIPMENT: small and medium heatproof bowls, whisk, small baking tray, 18 paper or foil minicups

1 ¼ CUPS CONFECTIONERS' SUGAR

2 OUNCES (½ STICK) UNSALTED BUTTER,
    CUT INTO SMALL PIECES

1 EGG WHITE

⅛ TEASPOON SALT

1 ¼ CUPS (5 OUNCES) COCONUT
    (UNSWEETENED OR SWEETENED),
    PACKED

1 ½ TEASPOONS VANILLA EXTRACT

4 OUNCES SEMISWEET OR MILK
    CHOCOLATE, CUT INTO SMALL PIECES*

1. Make the coconut filling: In a medium heatproof bowl set over a pan of simmering water, whisk together the confectioners' sugar, butter, egg white, and salt until very liquid and warm to the touch, about 10 minutes.

2. Remove from the heat and, with a spoon, stir in the coconut and vanilla until well combined. Cover with plastic wrap and refrigerate for 1 to 2 hours, up to overnight.

3. When ready to coat the coconut, in a small heatproof bowl set over a pan of simmering water melt the chocolate. When almost melted, turn off the heat and let the chocolate continue to melt completely, stirring occasionally. Keep the bowl over the warm water.

4. Form the balls: Line a small tray with parchment paper. Using a scant ounce of the coconut mixture, roll into a small ball and place on the parchment-lined tray. Repeat with the remaining mixture, forming 18 balls.

*If using milk chocolate, add 1 teaspoon of vegetable oil while melting.

5. Arrange 18 paper or foil minicups on the tray. Gently place one of the balls into the warm melted chocolate and, using two forks, roll the ball in the chocolate until well coated. Lift (do not pierce) the coated coconut ball with one of the forks, allowing some of the chocolate to drip back into the bowl, and carefully place in one of the prepared cups. Repeat with the remaining coconut balls and melted chocolate. Refrigerate until the chocolate has hardened and use as desired.

TO PREPARE AHEAD: Through step 5, the rounds can be prepared ahead and will keep for at least 1 week, refrigerated in a covered container.

PEANUT BUTTER CUPS

These creamy chocolate peanut butter cups literally melt in your mouth. You may want to cover half the peanut butter balls with semisweet chocolate and half with milk chocolate. When spooning out the chocolate, you can fill the cups to the very top or just to cover the peanut butter. The recipe can also be doubled, if desired.

EQUIPMENT: medium bowl, rubber spatula, medium heatproof bowl, 28 paper or foil minicups, baking tray

PEANUT BUTTER MIXTURE
1 CUP CREAMY PEANUT BUTTER
1 CUP CONFECTIONERS' SUGAR, SIFTED
1½ OUNCES (3 TABLESPOONS) VERY SOFT
    UNSALTED BUTTER, CUT INTO SMALL
    PIECES

1 TABLESPOON MILK
1 TABLESPOON VANILLA EXTRACT
½ TEASPOON SALT

• • •

12 OUNCES SEMISWEET OR MILK
    CHOCOLATE, CUT INTO SMALL PIECES*

1. Make the peanut butter mixture: In a medium bowl, combine the peanut butter, sugar, butter, milk, vanilla, and salt. Using a rubber spatula, blend together until very smooth. Cover and refrigerate for at least 1 hour.

2. In a medium heatproof bowl set over a pan of simmering water, melt the chocolate. When almost melted, turn off the heat and let the chocolate continue to melt completely, stirring occasionally. Keep the bowl over the warm water.

3. Make the peanut butter balls: Arrange 28 paper or foil minicups on a baking tray. Roll ½ ounce of the peanut butter mixture into a smooth ball and set into one of the cups. Repeat with the remaining mixture and cups.

4. Using a small spoon, carefully spoon the melted chocolate into each cup, covering each peanut butter ball, filling the cup as desired. Refrigerate until set, about 1 hour.

TO PREPARE AHEAD: Through step 4, the cups can be prepared and will keep at least 2 weeks, refrigerated in a covered container.

*If using milk chocolate, add 1 tablespoon of vegetable oil while melting.

CHOCOLATE-DIPPED ORANGE CREAMS

Makes 33 to 35 candies

The combination of orange and chocolate brings out the best in each flavor.

EQUIPMENT: electric mixer with large bowl, sifter, rolling pin, baking tray, 1-inch cookie cutter, small heatproof bowl

2 OUNCES (4 TABLESPOONS) UNSALTED BUTTER, AT ROOM TEMPERATURE, CUT INTO SMALL PIECES
1/3 CUP LIGHT CORN SYRUP
1 1/2 TEASPOONS ORANGE OIL OR ORANGE EXTRACT

4 CUPS CONFECTIONERS' SUGAR, SIFTED
ABOUT 4 OUNCES BITTERSWEET OR MILK CHOCOLATE

1. In the large bowl of an electric mixer fitted with a paddle or beaters, on medium speed, combine the butter, corn syrup, and orange oil. Beat until smooth and creamy.

2. Turn the speed to low and gradually add the sugar, 2 cups at a time, until the mixture starts to come together. Remove the mixture from the bowl and place on a work surface that has been lightly sprinkled with sifted confectioners' sugar. "Knead" the mixture until it is a smooth ball. If it is sticky, add a bit more confectioners' sugar. Don't add too much at one time; you want the mixture to stay creamy, and not be dry. Roll out to an 8-inch circle, about 1/2 inch thick. Cover with a clean towel and allow to rest for 30 minutes. Do not refrigerate.

3. Place a sheet of wax paper on a baking tray. Using a 1-inch cookie cutter, cut out 27 or 28 1-inch rounds. Reroll the "dough" to a 1/2-inch-thick circle and cut out 6 or 7 more rounds. Arrange the cut-out rounds on the prepared baking tray until needed.

4. Meanwhile, in a small heatproof bowl set over a pan of simmering water, temper the chocolate (see page 225). When the chocolate has reached the proper temperature, using a fork or truffle dipper, carefully dip the bottom half of each round of orange cream into the chocolate. As each orange cream is dipped into the chocolate, return it to the sheet of wax paper to set. Do not remove the candies from the paper until they are completely set.

TO PREPARE AHEAD: Prepare through step 4. To store, the creams can be placed between layers of wax paper in an airtight plastic container.

CHOCOLATE-ALMOND TOFFEE

Makes a 2-pound block,
10 × 13 inches

When you crave a sweet, this is perfect. The toffee, crushed, is folded into and sprinkled over our Spago's Toffee Tortoni (see page 182). It can be broken into larger pieces, wrapped, and stored in a cool spot.

EQUIPMENT: 1 or 2 baking trays, 11 × 15 inches, offset spatula, small deep saucepan, candy thermometer, long-handled wooden spoon, medium heatproof bowl

10 OUNCES WHOLE UNBLANCHED ALMONDS	**1 TEASPOON SALT**
1¼ CUPS GRANULATED SUGAR	**½ TEASPOON BAKING SODA**
⅓ CUP LIGHT CORN SYRUP	**8 OUNCES BITTERSWEET CHOCOLATE, CUT INTO SMALL PIECES**
⅓ CUP WATER OR RUM	
8 OUNCES (2 STICKS) UNSALTED BUTTER, CUT INTO SMALL PIECES	

1. Position the rack in the center of the oven and preheat the oven to 375 degrees.

2. Spread the nuts on a baking tray and bake until toasted, 10 to 15 minutes, turning the nuts after 7 or 8 minutes to ensure even toasting. Cool and then finely chop. You should have about 2 cups. Set aside. Clean the baking tray. Coat the baking tray and both sides of an offset spatula with vegetable spray. Set aside.

3. Make the toffee: Place the sugar in a small deep saucepan. Add the corn syrup and water, and over medium heat, bring to a boil. Let boil until large bubbles form on the surface, 3 to 4 minutes. Cover with foil or a lid and boil 5 minutes longer.

4. Add the pieces of butter and continue cooking, uncovered, over medium heat until the temperature reaches 300 degrees on a candy thermometer, about 30 minutes. (The candy thermometer has a clip on the side that can be slid up or down. If desired, you can fit it on the side of the pan, making sure that the thermometer rests *in* the mixture, not on the bottom of the pan, so that the reading is accurate.) Remove from the heat and immediately add the salt, baking soda, and 1 cup of the chopped nuts. Stir with a wooden spoon until well combined.

5. Pour the toffee mixture on the prepared baking tray and, using the offset spatula, spread the mixture out, making a block about 10 × 13 inches. The toffee will thicken very quickly, so work as fast as you can. When it's cool, blot some of the excess vegetable spray with a clean towel.

6. While the toffee mixture is cooling, in a medium heatproof bowl set over a pan of simmering water, melt the chocolate. When almost melted, turn off the heat and let the chocolate continue to melt, stirring occasionally. Keep warm.

7. When you can pick up the block of toffee in one piece, transfer it to a flat work surface or to a clean baking tray. Pour the melted chocolate over the toffee, spreading to cover the entire block of toffee. Before the chocolate cools, sprinkle the remaining chopped nuts over the chocolate. Refrigerate for about 10 minutes to set the chocolate.

8. Return the block of toffee to the work surface and break it up into pieces, approximately 1 to 1½ inches wide. Then cut into smaller pieces, as desired. Use as needed.

TO PREPARE AHEAD: Through step 8, store the toffee in a covered container. Keep in a cool spot.

SPAGO CHOCOLATE

SOUFFLÉS, BRÛLÉES, POTS DE CRÈMES, AND OTHER CREAMY DESSERTS

CLASSIC CHOCOLATE SOUFFLÉ 137

BLACK FOREST CHOCOLATE SOUFFLÉ 139

WHITE CHOCOLATE SOUFFLÉ WITH GRAND MARNIER SAUCE 141

HEAVENLY BANANA SOUFFLÉ SURPRISE 143

SPAGO CHOCOLATE ZABAIONE 146

MOCHA CRÈME BRÛLÉE 148

VANILLA CRÈME BRÛLÉE 150

DARK CHOCOLATE POT DE CRÈME 151

DARK CHOCOLATE POT DE CRÈME AND ORANGE BRÛLÉE 153

WHITE CHOCOLATE POT DE CRÈME AND GINGER BRÛLÉE 155

CHOCOLATE TRIFLE 157

CHOCOLATE TIRAMISÙ 160

Soufflé comes from the French verb *souffler,* which means "to blow or to breathe," hinting of the delicacy of the perfect soufflé. It consists of two important elements: the foundation, which gives the soufflé its flavor, and the whipped egg whites, which give it its light, airy texture. Because the soufflés in this book all contain chocolate, no starch (flour or arrowroot) is used in the recipes; chocolate contains enough starch to secure a firm base.

Making a soufflé is actually quite simple. Though many people are intimidated by them, nothing could be easier, and the result is most impressive. The tricky part is serving—soufflés *must* be served as soon as they come out of the oven. They cannot wait for the guests; the guests must wait for the soufflés.

To achieve a soufflé that has a somewhat crusty outer border and a creamy center, bake in a hot (400 degrees) oven. For a soufflé that is evenly cooked throughout, bake in a more moderate (325 degrees) oven. Always bake the soufflé on the lowest rack in the oven. Do not open the oven door during the baking process or it may collapse—wait until the soufflé is almost ready to come out of the oven and then check it.

To prepare the baking dish(es), brush with melted butter and invert them on a tray so that any excess butter will run off. Then, spoon some granulated sugar into the dish and rotate to coat the bottom and sides with the sugar. If using more than one dish, pour any excess sugar into the next dish, repeating the rotating procedure, again pouring the excess sugar into any remaining dishes. Check to make sure each dish is properly coated with sugar; you may have to brush a little more butter around and sprinkle a little more sugar over.

Spooning, rather than pouring, the batter into the dish will make for an airier soufflé. Use a large spoon and fill the dish to the very top. The batter can be level or mounded.

Uncooked soufflés can be frozen. If freezing, make sure you use dishes that can go from freezer to oven without cracking or breaking. (We recommend Corning Ware dishes.) Wrap the soufflé well and place on a level spot in your freezer. Baking should be almost twice as long as specified in the original recipe, depending on how deeply frozen it is. If the original time is 9 to 10 minutes, check after 18 minutes. If the top is puffy and nicely browned, the soufflé should be ready.

To serve, break into the top of each soufflé with a small spoon and spoon the desired sauce(s) into the opening. Fruit can be passed, with guests helping themselves, or used to decorate each plate.

All the desserts in this chapter have an egg base, some with yolks, some with whole eggs, all light in texture. Though rich, a small amount goes a long way. These desserts will please even the most critical and difficult palate.

. . .

CLASSIC CHOCOLATE SOUFFLÉ

Serves 6

The grandfather of dessert soufflés! When folding the whites into the basic mixture, it is important not to overmix. Overmixing will make the egg whites deflate and you won't get the proper consistency for a light soufflé. (If we repeat ourselves, it's to make an important point.) Finely chopped orange zest can be added for additional flavor. When serving with a sauce, it is best spooned into the soufflé at the table.

EQUIPMENT: six ¾-cup ovenproof soufflé dishes, flat baking tray, small heatproof bowl, electric mixer with 2 large bowls, large spoon

6 OUNCES BITTERSWEET CHOCOLATE, CUT INTO SMALL PIECES

3 EGG YOLKS

½ CUP GRANULATED SUGAR

1 TEASPOON VANILLA EXTRACT

5 EGG WHITES

SIFTED CONFECTIONERS' SUGAR

WHIPPED CREAM OR DRAMBUIE-FLAVORED CRÈME ANGLAISE (SEE PAGE 205)

1. Position the rack in the lowest part of the oven and preheat the oven to 400 degrees. Brush six ¾-cup ovenproof soufflé dishes with melted butter and invert the dishes to allow excess butter to drip out. Then, pour a little granulated sugar into each dish, turning to coat all sides, tapping out any excess sugar (see page 134). For easier handling, arrange the dishes on a flat baking tray and set aside.

2. In a small heatproof bowl placed over a pan of simmering water, melt the chocolate. When almost melted, turn off the heat and let the chocolate melt completely, stirring occasionally.

3. Meanwhile, in the large bowl of an electric mixer fitted with a paddle or beaters, on high speed beat together the egg yolks, ¼ cup plus 2 tablespoons of the sugar, and the vanilla until pale yellow and thick. Scrape the melted chocolate into the yolks and continue to beat until well combined.

4. In another clean large bowl, with whip or clean beaters, whip the 5 egg whites. Start on medium speed and raise the speed as peaks begin to form. Add the remaining 2 tablespoons sugar and continue to whip until the whites are shiny and firm, but not stiff. (When the bowl is tipped slightly, the whites should stay in place.) Stir one-

third of the whites into the chocolate mixture to lighten, then turn the chocolate back into the whites and fold until completely incorporated. *Do not overmix.*

5. Using a large spoon, spoon the soufflé batter into the prepared dishes, filling to the top of each dish. Bake 10 minutes; the tops will be slightly crusty and the inside creamy.

6. To serve, carefully remove each soufflé and place on a small doily-lined plate. Dust with sifted confectioner's sugar and serve with softly whipped cream or Drambuie-Flavored Crème Anglaise. Serve immediately.

TO PREPARE AHEAD: Do not prepare ahead, unless you are freezing the soufflés (see pages 134–35).

BLACK FOREST CHOCOLATE SOUFFLÉ

The inspiration for this soufflé comes from the Black Forest cake that has been so popular over the years. This should be made only when cherries are in season and bursting with flavor.

EQUIPMENT: six ¾-cup ovenproof soufflé dishes, flat baking tray, small nonreactive saucepan, slotted spoon, small heatproof bowl, electric mixer with 2 large bowls, rubber spatula, large spoon

¾ **POUND FRESH CHERRIES, STEMMED, PITTED, AND CUT IN HALF**	**5 OUNCES BITTERSWEET CHOCOLATE, CUT INTO SMALL PIECES**
½ **CUP KIRSCH OR CHERRY LIQUEUR**	**3 EGG YOLKS**
1 CUP GRANULATED SUGAR	**5 EGG WHITES**

1. Position the rack in the lowest part of the oven and preheat the oven to 400 degrees. Brush six ¾-cup ovenproof soufflé dishes with melted butter and invert the dishes to allow excess butter to drip out. Then, pour a little granulated sugar into each dish, turning to coat all sides, tapping out any excess sugar (see page 134). For easier handling, arrange the dishes on a flat baking tray and set aside.

2. In a small nonreactive saucepan, soak the cherries in the kirsch or cherry liqueur for about 30 minutes, turning to coat with the liquid. Add ½ cup of the sugar and cook over medium heat until the cherries are softened, 15 to 20 minutes. Remove the cherries with a slotted spoon and continue to heat the juices until ½ cup remains. Set aside.

3. In a small heatproof bowl set over a pan of simmering water, melt the chocolate. When almost melted, turn off the heat and let the chocolate melt completely, stirring occasionally. Stir in 2 teaspoons of the warm cherry juice.

4. Meanwhile, in the large bowl of an electric mixer fitted with a paddle or beaters, on high speed (or in a large bowl, using a whisk by hand), beat together the 3 egg yolks and ¼ cup plus 2 tablespoons of the sugar until pale yellow and thick. Scrape in the melted chocolate and continue to beat until well combined.

5. In another clean large bowl, with a whip or beaters, whip the 5 egg whites. Start on

139

medium speed and raise the speed as peaks begin to form. Add the remaining 2 tablespoons of sugar and continue to whip until the whites are shiny and firm, but not stiff. (When the bowl is tipped slightly, the whites should stay in place.) Stir one-third of the whites into the chocolate mixture to lighten, then turn the chocolate into the whites and, with a rubber spatula, fold until completely incorporated. *Do not overmix.*

6. Place four or five cherry halves on the bottom of each soufflé dish. Using a large spoon, spoon the soufflé batter into the prepared dishes, filling to the top of each dish. Bake 10 to 11 minutes; the tops will be slightly crusty and the inside creamy.

7. Meanwhile, return the remaining cherries to the saucepan containing the cherry juice and reheat.

8. To serve, carefully remove each soufflé and place on a small doily-lined plate. Dust the top with confectioners' sugar and serve with cherries, sauce, and whipped cream.

TO PREPARE AHEAD: Do not prepare ahead, unless you are freezing the soufflés (see pages 134–35).

WHITE CHOCOLATE SOUFFLÉ

WITH GRAND MARNIER SAUCE

Serves 4

This is a delicate-tasting soufflé. White chocolate has a subtle flavor that goes particularly well with this sauce. If you do not want to serve it with a sauce, sift unsweetened cocoa powder over the top just before serving.

EQUIPMENT: six ¾-cup ovenproof soufflé dishes, flat baking tray, small heatproof bowl, electric mixer with 2 large bowls, large spoon

½ CUP HEAVY CREAM	¼ CUP GRANULATED SUGAR
1 TABLESPOON GRAND MARNIER	ZEST OF 1 LARGE ORANGE, CHOPPED FINE
6 OUNCES WHITE CHOCOLATE, CUT	(2 TABLESPOONS PLUS 2 TEASPOONS)
INTO SMALL PIECES	5 EGG WHITES
3 EGG YOLKS	GRAND MARNIER SAUCE (SEE PAGE 204)

1. Position the rack in the lowest part of the oven and preheat the oven to 400 degrees. Brush six ¾-cup ovenproof soufflé dishes with melted butter and invert the dishes to allow excess butter to drip out. Then, pour a little granulated sugar into each dish, turning to coat all sides, removing any excess sugar (see page 134). For easier handling, arrange the dishes on a flat baking tray and set aside.

2. In a small heatproof bowl set over a pan of simmering water, heat the cream and Grand Marnier. Add the chocolate. When almost melted, turn off the heat and let melt completely, stirring occasionally.

3. Meanwhile, in the large bowl of an electric mixer fitted with a paddle or beaters, on high speed beat the egg yolks and 2 tablespoons of the sugar until pale yellow and thick. Lower the speed and scrape in the chocolate mixture. Continue to beat until well combined. Remove the bowl from the machine and stir in the orange zest.

4. In another clean large bowl, with a whip or clean beaters, whip the 5 egg whites. Start on medium speed and raise the speed as peaks begin to form. Add the remaining 2 tablespoons of sugar and continue to whip until the whites are shiny and firm, but not stiff. (When the bowl is tipped slightly, the whites should stay in place.)

Stir one-third of the whites into the chocolate mixture to lighten, then turn the chocolate mixture into the whites and fold until completely incorporated. *Do not overmix.*

5. Using a large spoon, spoon the soufflé batter into the prepared dishes, filling to the top of each dish. Bake 9 to 10 minutes; the top will be browned and slightly crusty and the inside creamy.

6. To serve, carefully remove each soufflé and place on a small doily-lined plate. Pass the Grand Marnier Sauce.

TO PREPARE AHEAD: Do not prepare ahead unless you are freezing the soufflés (see pages 134–35).

HEAVENLY BANANA SOUFFLÉ SURPRISE

Serves 6

This tastes like nothing you've eaten on this earth. The chocolate melts into the soufflé, blending with the banana, giving this soufflé its distinctive flavor. The bananas for this soufflé should be very ripe for the best result. When bananas are ripe, they can be mashed with a fork.

EQUIPMENT: six ¾-cup ovenproof soufflé dishes, flat baking tray, large bowl, medium bowl, whisk, electric mixer with large bowl, large rubber spatula, large spoon, sifter

1 LARGE OR 2 MEDIUM (5 OUNCES) RIPE BANANAS	1 TEASPOON VANILLA EXTRACT
1 TABLESPOON BANANA LIQUEUR*	3 OUNCES BITTERSWEET CHOCOLATE, COARSELY CHOPPED
3 EGG YOLKS	SIFTED UNSWEETENED COCOA POWDER
⅓ CUP GRANULATED SUGAR	SIFTED CONFECTIONERS' SUGAR
5 EGG WHITES	

1. Place the rack in the lowest part of the oven and preheat the oven to 400 degrees. Brush six ¾-cup ovenproof soufflé dishes with melted butter and invert so that excess butter will run off. Coat well with granulated sugar, tapping out any excess sugar (see page 134). Arrange the dishes on a flat baking tray and set aside.

2. Puree the bananas and place in a large bowl. Pour the banana liqueur over and mix well. Set aside.

3. In a medium bowl, using a whisk, whip the egg yolks with 2 tablespoons of the sugar until pale yellow. Stir into the bananas and combine thoroughly.

4. In the large bowl of an electric mixer fitted with a whip or beaters, on medium speed whip the 5 egg whites until frothy. Add the remaining sugar and the vanilla, turn the speed to high, and beat until the whites are thick and shiny and hold their shape. (When the bowl is tipped slightly, the whites should stay in place.)

---

* If you prefer, you can substitute lemon juice for the banana liqueur.

143

5. Stir a little of the whites into the banana mixture to lighten, then turn the mixture back into the whites and fold through quickly and completely with a large rubber spatula. *Do not overmix.* This will make the egg whites deflate and you won't get the proper consistency for a light soufflé. Using a large spoon, spoon the batter into the prepared soufflé dishes, half filling each one. Divide the chocolate, place in the middle of the batter in each dish, and continue filling each dish to the very top.

6. Bake 11 minutes. The tops will be slightly firm and lightly browned. Remove from the oven and sift a little cocoa powder and then confectioners' sugar over the tops.

7. To serve, place each dish on a small doily-lined dessert plate and immediately bring to the table. If you like, you can pass a bowl of unsweetened whipped cream.

TO PREPARE AHEAD: Through step 5, soufflés can be frozen (see pages 134–35).

SPAGO CHOCOLATE ZABAIONE

Serves 5 to 6

At Spago, we jazz up zabaione with chocolate liqueur and fold in a little whipped cream. Zabaione can be served warm or chilled. We serve it chilled, spooned into goblets.

EQUIPMENT: medium bowl, whisk or eggbeater, large heatproof bowl, sifter, rubber spatula, large spoon, flat baking tray

⅔ CUP HEAVY CREAM

8 EGG YOLKS

½ CUP GRANULATED SUGAR

6 TABLESPOONS UNSWEETENED COCOA
POWDER, SIFTED

3 TABLESPOONS GODIVA CHOCOLATE
LIQUEUR, OR ANY GOOD-QUALITY
CHOCOLATE LIQUEUR

1. In a medium bowl, using a whisk or eggbeater, whip the cream until soft peaks form. Cover and refrigerate until needed.

2. In a large heatproof bowl set over a pan of barely simmering water, whisk together the egg yolks and sugar until the yolks are warm to the touch and the sugar is completely dissolved. Remove from the heat and whisk in the cocoa until smooth. Cool slightly.

3. Whisk in the chocolate liqueur, then with a rubber spatula fold in the reserved whipped cream. Spoon into five or six serving goblets or dishes of your choice. Set the serving dishes on a flat baking tray and refrigerate, covered, 2 to 3 hours, or until ready to serve.

4. To serve, spoon a dollop of whipped cream on top and decorate with shaved chocolate.

TO PREPARE AHEAD: Through step 3, the Zabaione can be prepared early in the day it is to be served.

VARIATION: To make Mocha Zabaione, substitute 4 tablespoons cocoa and 2 tablespoons instant espresso for the 6 tablespoons cocoa. Substitute Grand Marnier for the chocolate liqueur.

MOCHA CRÈME BRÛLÉE

Serves 6 to 8

Makes about 3 cups

This crème brûlée is very smooth and rich, and a small amount can be incredibly satisfying. It can be made in pot de crème cups or demitasse (espresso) cups.

EQUIPMENT: rolling pin, medium heavy saucepan, wooden spoon, medium heatproof bowl, whisk, fine-mesh strainer, large bowl plus a slightly larger bowl, six 4-ounce cups or eight 3-ounce cups, flat baking tray, propane torch (optional; see page 222)

½ CUP DECAFFEINATED ESPRESSO BEANS

1½ CUPS HEAVY CREAM

6 OUNCES BITTERSWEET CHOCOLATE,
CUT INTO SMALL PIECES

10 EGG YOLKS

⅓ CUP GRANULATED SUGAR PLUS
ADDITIONAL TO CARAMELIZE TOPS

1. Crush the espresso beans. The easiest method is to loosely enclose the beans in a plastic bag and then crush by rolling a rolling pin over the beans several times. (Or you can use a food processor fitted with a steel blade. Crush with a few on/off turns. You do not want the beans crushed too fine.) Transfer the beans to a medium heavy saucepan, pour the cream over, and stir with a wooden spoon. Bring to a boil, add the chocolate bits, and remove from the heat. Let steep 15 minutes, stirring occasionally, to dissolve the chocolate. Keep warm.

2. Meanwhile, in a medium heatproof bowl whisk together the egg yolks and sugar. Set the bowl over a pan of barely simmering water and continue to whisk vigorously until the mixture becomes a very pale yellow and feels hot to the touch and is very thick. (It is important to whisk as long as the eggs are over the heat to prevent "scrambling" the eggs.) Do not rush this; keep on low to medium heat.

3. Bring the cream back to a boil and whisk into the egg mixture, whisking until completely incorporated. Strain through a fine-mesh strainer into a clean bowl and set the bowl in a larger bowl or basin. Fill the larger bowl with ice cubes and water that reaches about halfway up the sides of the smaller bowl. Whisk occasionally until it cools.

4. Spoon into six 4-ounce cups or eight 3-ounce cups. The mixture must come to the edge of the cups so that the tops can be caramelized. Set the cups on a flat baking tray and refrigerate until needed, 2 to 3 hours.

5. When ready to serve, sprinkle 1 or 2 teaspoons granulated sugar around the top of each serving. Using a propane torch, caramelize the sugar to a golden brown.* If not caramelized enough, sprinkle with a little more sugar and torch again. Serve immediately with a few fresh raspberries.

TO PREPARE AHEAD: Through step 4, the brûlée can be made early in the day it is being served.

> * If you don't feel comfortable using a torch, you can eliminate this step and just serve topped with a dollop of whipped cream.

VANILLA CRÈME BRÛLÉE

Makes about 3 cups

This is an incredibly versatile dessert. You can serve the brûlée in shallow soufflé dishes or ramekins, caramelized with a propane torch (see Mocha Crème Brûlée, page 149); just sprinkle a little granulated sugar over the tops and torch. You may need a few layers of sugar for an overall caramelized coating. The vanilla cream also makes an intensely delicious cake filling or fruit topping. When Mary was on Julia Child's series, *Baking with Julia,* she made a chocolate chiffon bundt cake with fruit and vanilla cream. It was sheer decadence.

EQUIPMENT: heavy medium saucepan, medium heatproof bowl, whisk, large bowl plus a slightly larger bowl, fine-mesh strainer, propane torch (optional; see page 222)

1½ CUPS HEAVY CREAM	10 EGG YOLKS
1 VANILLA BEAN, SPLIT LENGTHWISE	⅓ CUP GRANULATED SUGAR

1. In a heavy medium saucepan, combine the cream and the vanilla bean with its scrapings. Over low heat, bring just to a boil.

2. In a medium heatproof bowl, whisk together the egg yolks and sugar. Place over a pan of barely simmering water and continue to whisk vigorously until the mixture becomes a very pale yellow and feels hot to the touch and is very thick. (It is important to whisk as long as the eggs are over the heat to prevent "scrambling" the eggs.) Do not rush this; keep on medium heat.

3. Remove from the heat and immediately whisk in the boiling cream. Transfer the bowl back over the saucepan, but do *not* turn on the heat. Whisk the mixture occasionally until it thickens, about 10 minutes.

4. When the mixture thickens, place the bowl in a basin or larger bowl filled with cold water and ice cubes. Whisk occasionally until cool. Strain through a fine-mesh strainer into a clean bowl and refrigerate, covered, until needed.

TO PREPARE AHEAD: Through step 4, the brûlée can be made early in the day it is being served.

DARK CHOCOLATE POT DE CRÈME

People often confuse pot de crème with chocolate pudding, but there is really no comparison. This is much smoother, richer, and infinitely more delicious. There are special pot de crème cups that come with their own lids, which of course makes a very attractive presentation, but ramekins will do just as well.

EQUIPMENT: 2 medium heatproof bowls, medium saucepan, whisk, fine-mesh strainer, ladle, six ¾-cup ramekins, baking pan with sides, large enough to hold ramekins, flat baking pan

3 OUNCES BITTERSWEET CHOCOLATE, CUT INTO SMALL PIECES	**5 EGG YOLKS**
2 CUPS HEAVY CREAM	**¼ CUP GRANULATED SUGAR**
½ CUP MILK	**PINCH OF SALT**

1. Position the rack in the center of the oven and preheat the oven to 325 degrees.

2. In a medium heatproof bowl set over a pan of gently simmering water, heat the chocolate. When the chocolate is almost melted, turn off the heat and let stand until completely melted, stirring occasionally.

3. Meanwhile, in a medium saucepan, scald the cream and milk.

4. In another medium heatproof bowl, whisk together the egg yolks, sugar, and salt until the sugar is completely dissolved. Slowly whisk the hot cream mixture into the yolks.

5. Remove the melted chocolate from the stove and pour the hot cream mixture through a fine-mesh strainer into the melted chocolate. Whisk until well combined and smooth.

6. Ladle the mixture into six ¾-cup ramekins and arrange the ramekins in a baking pan with sides. Pour in enough warm water to reach halfway up the sides of the ramekins, cover the entire pan with aluminum foil, and place in the oven. Bake until the mixture around the edges of each ramekin is firm when lightly shaken, about 35 minutes. (Baking time will vary depending upon the depth and width of the ramekins.) The center may still move a bit, but it will firm up as it chills.

7. Carefully remove the ramekins from the baking pan, wipe dry, and let cool. Place on a flat baking tray, cover with foil, and refrigerate until firm, 2 to 3 hours.

8. To serve, spoon a little whipped cream in the center of each serving and, if you like, top with a tiny candied violet. Set each cup on a small doily-lined dessert plate.

TO PREPARE AHEAD: Through step 7, the Pot de Crème can be prepared up to 1 day ahead.

DARK CHOCOLATE POT DE CRÈME
AND ORANGE BRÛLÉE

Serves 12

Here is an example of taking two distinct recipes for dessert—crème brûlée and pot de crème—and combining them to create a delightful new concoction. Traditionally, brûlée is sprinkled with granulated sugar and torched, caramelizing the sugar. If you object to using a propane torch in your kitchen, feel free to eliminate this step. Just spoon or pipe a little whipped cream over the top and serve with the orange segments.

EQUIPMENT: twelve ¾-cup ramekins, baking pan with sides, flat baking tray, zester, propane torch (optional; see page 222)

DARK CHOCOLATE POT DE CRÈME (SEE PAGE 151)	ZEST OF 5 MEDIUM ORANGES
VANILLA CRÈME BRÛLÉE (SEE PAGE 150)	ORANGE SEGMENTS, WHITE PITH COMPLETELY REMOVED

1. Position the rack in the center of the oven and preheat the oven to 325 degrees.

2. Make the Pot de Crème: Spoon into twelve ¾-cup ramekins, filling halfway up each ramekin. Arrange the ramekins in a baking pan with sides, then pour enough warm water into the baking pan to cover the bottoms of the ramekins. Cover the entire pan with aluminum foil and place in the oven. Bake until the mixture around the edges is firm when lightly shaken, about 20 minutes. The center may still move a bit, but it will firm up as it chills.

3. Carefully remove the ramekins from the baking pan, wipe dry, and let cool. Set on a flat baking tray, cover with aluminum foil, and refrigerate until firm, 2 to 3 hours.

4. Meanwhile, make the Orange Brûlée: Make the Vanilla Crème Brûlée as directed and in step 3, add the zest to the pot while the cream is coming to a boil. Remove from the heat and let steep at least 30 minutes before continuing with the recipe. When cold, spoon over the chilled pot de crème, filling each ramekin to the top. Return to the refrigerator until needed.

5. To serve, sprinkle the tops with granulated sugar and, using a propane torch, caramelize the brûlée to a golden brown. Arrange a few orange segments on the brûlée and serve immediately.

TO PREPARE AHEAD: Through step 3, the Pot de Crème can be made 1 day ahead. The brûlée should be made early the day it is being served. Caramelize it just before serving.

WHITE CHOCOLATE POT DE CRÈME AND GINGER BRÛLÉE

This is a double whammy: The sweetness of the white chocolate is balanced by the bite of the ginger. When making the ginger brûlée, it is important to let the ginger steep in the hot cream until the desired flavor is obtained. If you prefer not to torch the brûlée, you may want to sprinkle a little chopped crystallized ginger over the top.

EQUIPMENT: 2 medium heatproof bowls, medium saucepan, whisk, fine-mesh strainer, ladle, twelve ¾-cup ramekins, baking pan with sides, flat baking tray, propane torch, optional

POT DE CRÈME
3 OUNCES WHITE CHOCOLATE, CUT INTO SMALL PIECES
2 CUPS HEAVY CREAM
½ CUP MILK
1 VANILLA BEAN, SPLIT LENGTHWISE AND SCRAPED
5 EGG YOLKS
2 TABLESPOONS GRANULATED SUGAR

PINCH OF SALT
1½ TABLESPOONS KAHLÚA, FRAMBOISE, OR GRAND MARNIER

GINGER BRÛLÉE
VANILLA CRÈME BRÛLÉE (SEE PAGE 150)
SIX ½-INCH SLICES OF PEELED FRESH GINGER

1. Make the Pot de Crème: Position the rack in the center of the oven and preheat the oven to 325 degrees.

2. In a medium heatproof bowl set over a pan of barely simmering water, melt the chocolate. When the chocolate is almost melted, turn off the heat and let it stand until completely melted, stirring occasionally.

3. In a medium saucepan, scald the cream and milk with the scraped vanilla bean. Turn off the heat and let it steep for 15 minutes, then bring back to a boil.

4. Meanwhile, in another medium heatproof bowl, whisk together the egg yolks, sugar, and salt until the sugar is completely dissolved. Slowly whisk the hot cream mixture into the yolks. Pour through a fine-mesh strainer into the melted chocolate and whisk

until well combined and smooth. Stir in the liqueur of your choice and ladle into twelve ¾-cup ramekins, filling halfway up each ramekin. Arrange the ramekins in a baking pan with sides, then pour enough warm water into the baking pan to cover the bottoms of the ramekins. Cover the entire pan with aluminum foil, seal around the pan, and place in the oven. Bake until the edges around the Pot de Crème are firm when lightly shaken, about 20 minutes. (To do this, slowly pull out the rack, holding the pan barely out of the oven, and carefully lift the foil.) The center may still move a bit, but it will firm up as it chills.

5. Carefully remove the ramekins from the baking pan, wipe dry, and let cool. Set on a flat baking tray and refrigerate until firm, 2 to 3 hours.

6. Make the Ginger Brûlée: Make the Vanilla Crème Brûlée and in step 1, add the pieces of ginger to the pot while the cream is coming to a boil. Turn off the heat and let steep at least 30 minutes. Then continue with the recipe. When cold, spoon over the chilled Pot de Crème, filling each ramekin to the top. Return to the refrigerator until needed.

7. To serve, sprinkle a little granulated sugar over the top of each brûlée and caramelize with a propane torch. This may have to be repeated until you have the desired color. Then set the ramekins on small doily-lined dessert plates and serve immediately.

TO PREPARE AHEAD: Through step 5, the Pot de Crème can be made 1 day ahead. The brûlée should be made early the next day and torched when ready to serve.

CHOCOLATE TRIFLE

In the restaurant, we serve trifle in individual goblets. If it's easier for you, you can assemble it in an attractive glass bowl or trifle dish. The beauty of this dish is in the layers, which should be visible. When in season, raspberries, blackberries, or a combination can be substituted for the strawberries. Cook as described below, but strain before spooning into the trifle, pressing down on the berries as you strain them, returning a few of the seeds to the berry compote, if desired, for texture, stirring to combine.

EQUIPMENT: small nonreactive saucepan, zester, small cup, six 8-ounce goblets

2 TO 2½ CUPS VANILLA PASTRY CREAM (SEE PAGE 194)

½ LOAF (8 OUNCES) CHOCOLATE BRIOCHE (SEE PAGE 73)

2 PINTS STRAWBERRIES, STEMMED, PLUS ADDITIONAL STRAWBERRIES AS GARNISH

1 CUP GRANULATED SUGAR

ZEST AND JUICE OF 1 MEDIUM ORANGE

¼ CUP GRAND MARNIER

¼ CUP CHAMBORD

GRATED MILK CHOCOLATE, OPTIONAL

1. Prepare the pastry cream and refrigerate overnight.

2. Make the brioche the day before. When ready to make the trifle, cut the brioche into cubes, about 1 inch thick. (You do not have to remove the crust.) You should have about 4 cups. Set aside.

3. Make the strawberry compote: If the berries are large, cut them in half or slices. In a small nonreactive saucepan, combine the berries, sugar, zest, and juice. Cook over medium heat until the compote begins to thicken, skimming off the scum as it forms on the top, 10 to 15 minutes. Let cool completely. (The compote will thicken even more as it cools.)

4. In a small cup, combine the Grand Marnier and Chambord. Set aside.

5. Assemble the trifle: For each trifle, place a few brioche cubes in the bottom of an 8-ounce goblet and sprinkle with a little of the combined liqueurs (about 2 teaspoons).

Spoon about 3 tablespoons pastry cream over the bread, top with about 1 1/2 table-spoons strawberry compote, another layer of bread cubes, a sprinkling of liqueurs, about 2 tablespoons pastry cream, compote, and a last layer of pastry cream, about 1 1/2 tablespoons. You will have two layers of brioche cubes, three layers of pastry cream, and two layers of compote. Repeat with the remaining bread cubes, liqueurs, pastry cream, and compote, filling the remaining five goblets. Refrigerate for 2 hours, up to 6 hours.

6. To serve, place each goblet on a small doily-lined plate. Grate a little milk chocolate over the pastry cream, if desired, and top with a whole, fanned strawberry and a mint sprig. Serve immediately.

TO PREPARE AHEAD: The brioche must be made 1 or 2 days before. Pastry cream should be made the day before. Through step 5, assemble the trifle early in the day.

CHOCOLATE TIRAMISÙ

When Mary made this for the TV Food Network show *Baker's Dozen,* she served it "family style" in a clear glass trifle bowl and spooned it into smaller bowls at the table. It can also be layered in individual serving dishes. At the restaurant, Mary used martini glasses. Keep in mind that we don't expect everyone to have the exact size we may use, so be a little creative with what you *do* have.

EQUIPMENT: 12 × 17 × 1-inch baking tray, long offset spatula, 2-, 2½-, and 2¾-inch round cookie cutters, large heatproof bowl, whisk, electric mixer with large bowl, medium bowl, 8 to 10 large goblets or large clear trifle bowl

CHOCOLATE CHIFFON CAKE
    (SEE PAGE 13)

MASCARPONE CREAM
6 EGGS, SEPARATED
2½ TABLESPOONS GRANULATED SUGAR
1 POUND MASCARPONE CHEESE
¼ CUP DARK RUM
2 TABLESPOONS KAHLÚA
4 OUNCES MILK CHOCOLATE, GRATED,
    PLUS EXTRA AS NEEDED

SOAKING LIQUID
2 CUPS STRONG HOT COFFEE, REGULAR
    OR DECAFFEINATED
½ CUP GRANULATED SUGAR
¼ CUP RUM
2 TABLESPOONS KAHLÚA
2 TABLESPOONS GRAND MARNIER

1. Prepare the cake batter as directed. Butter or coat with vegetable spray a 12 × 17 × 1-inch baking tray and line with parchment paper. Sprinkle with flour, invert the pan and tap to remove any excess flour. Position the rack in the center of the oven and preheat the oven to 350 degrees.

2. Scrape the batter into the prepared pan and even the top by running a long offset spatula across the surface. Bake until the cake springs back when lightly touched, about 15 minutes. Cool on a rack. When completely cool, with a sharp knife, cut around the edges of the cake, separating the cake from the pan. Invert the pan onto a firm, flat surface and gently peel away the parchment paper. Using cookie cutters, cut out eight 2-inch circles, eight 2½-inch circles, and eight 2¾-inch circles. Set aside.

3. While the cake is baking, make the mascarpone cream: In a large heatproof bowl set over a pan of simmering water, whisk the egg yolks and 2 tablespoons of the sugar until the sugar dissolves and the mixture is hot to the touch. Remove from the heat and whisk in the mascarpone. Set aside.

4. In the large bowl of an electric mixer fitted with whip or beaters, on medium speed beat the egg whites to soft peaks. Add the remaining $\frac{1}{2}$ tablespoon sugar, turn up the speed, and beat until shiny and firm but not stiff. Fold into the mascarpone mixture. Stir in the rum and Kahlúa, adding more as necessary to taste. Refrigerate, covered, until chilled, then fold in the grated chocolate. Return to the refrigerator until needed.

5. Make the soaking liquid: In a medium bowl, combine all the ingredients and mix well. Set aside and let cool.

6. Assemble the tiramisù: Dip each cake circle, one at a time, in the soaking liquid, until it is coated with liquid but still whole, gently squeezing out the excess liquid. Do not let the cake sit in the liquid too long, as it will fall apart. Place one cake circle at the bottom of a wide, tall glass (the glass should be wider at the top than at the bottom). Spoon some of the mascarpone cream into the glass, add a second cake circle, more cream, a third cake circle, and a last layer of cream. Repeat with the remaining glasses, mascarpone cream, and cake. Refrigerate 4 to 5 hours. When ready to serve, place each goblet on a small doily-lined dessert plate, sprinkle grated chocolate over the top and serve with a small biscotti or cookie. Serve immediately.

TO PREPARE AHEAD: Through step 2, the cake can be made one day ahead, wrapped well, and refrigerated. The mascarpone cream and soaking liquid can be made early in the day. The tiramisù should be assembled 4 to 5 hours ahead of serving time, allowing it to set.

FROZEN DESSERTS

ALMOND ICE CREAM WITH CHOCOLATE-DIPPED ALMONDS 165

APRICOT ICE CREAM 167

BANANA-CHOCOLATE CHIP ICE CREAM 169

BANANA SPLITS 171

CHOCOLATE-ALMOND ICE CREAM CAKE 172

CHOCOLATE TARTUFO 175

DAVID'S ORANGE-YOU-GLAD-IT'S-CHOCOLATE ICE CREAM 178

MILK CHOCOLATE ICE CREAM 180

PINEAPPLE ICE CREAM 181

CRUNCHY TOFFEE TORTONI 182

TÍA MARÍA-COFFEE ICE CREAM WITH FUDGE SWIRL 184

VANILLA LOW-FAT YOGURT 186

LOW-FAT FROZEN CHOCOLATE YOGURT 188

*T*he first frozen dessert, it has been said, originated in China, centuries ago. An extremely grateful Marco Polo brought his discovery to Italy. From there it traveled to other countries in Europe and eventually found its way to America, where the public embraced this delicacy with open arms (or rather, mouths).

At Spago Las Vegas, frozen desserts are incredibly popular. And they are not difficult to make. All you need is an ice cream maker—either the old-fashioned crank type or an electric model will do—and a little imagination. And ice cream cakes are great for birthday parties: you can eat your cake, and have your ice cream, too!

. . .

ALMOND ICE CREAM WITH

CHOCOLATE-DIPPED ALMONDS

Makes about 2 quarts

This is one of our favorite ice creams. We use two kinds of almonds in the recipe: Unblanched almonds have the skins on, and blanched almonds have the skins removed. We dip the unblanched almonds in the chocolate because they are more flavorful and won't be overwhelmed by the chocolate.

In step 3, allow the almonds to steep until you get as much of the flavor as possible. Let your taste be your guide. If you have a toaster oven, the almonds can be toasted on the baking tray.

EQUIPMENT: 2 small baking trays, large nonreactive saucepan, baking tray, medium heatproof bowl, large heatproof bowl plus a slightly larger bowl, whisk, fine-mesh strainer, long-handled wooden spoon, ice cream maker

2 CUPS (10 OUNCES) WHOLE BLANCHED ALMONDS	2 CUPS MILK
4 OUNCES WHOLE UNBLANCHED ALMONDS (WITH SKINS STILL ON)	2 OUNCES BITTERSWEET CHOCOLATE
2 CUPS HEAVY CREAM	8 EGG YOLKS
	½ CUP GRANULATED SUGAR

1. Position the rack in the center of the oven and preheat the oven to 350 degrees.

2. Spread the blanched and unblanched almonds on two separate small baking trays. Toast for 10 minutes, turning after 5 minutes. Coarsely chop the blanched almonds and set aside. Set aside the unblanched almonds.

3. In a large nonreactive saucepan, bring the cream and milk to a boil. Remove from the heat, stir in the chopped blanched almonds, and let steep, covered, until the liquid is very flavorful, about 1½ hours. Line a baking tray with parchment paper. Set aside.

4. Meanwhile, in a medium heatproof bowl set over a pan of simmering water, melt the chocolate with the unblanched toasted almonds, stirring occasionally to coat the nuts with the chocolate. When completely melted and coated, carefully spread the nuts

out onto the prepared baking tray to cool. Gently separate with the tines of a fork and refrigerate until needed.

5. In a large heatproof bowl, whisk the egg yolks. Gradually whisk in the sugar until thoroughly combined. Strain the cream mixture through a fine-mesh strainer, discarding the nuts, and slowly whisk the cream into the egg yolks. Return the mixture to the saucepan and over low heat, stirring constantly with a wooden spoon, cook until the mixture thickens enough to coat the back of the spoon. (If you run your finger down the back of the spoon, the mixture will not run together.) Pour the mixture back into the bowl, set the bowl into a slightly larger bowl filled with ice cubes and cold water, and chill about 30 minutes, replacing the ice cubes as they dissolve.

6. Strain into the bowl of an ice cream maker and freeze according to the manufacturer's directions. When almost frozen, gradually add the chocolate-coated nuts so that they are distributed throughout the ice cream. Scrape into a chilled container, cover with aluminum foil, and place in the freezer until needed. About 30 minutes before serving, transfer to the refrigerator.

7. To serve, place two small scoops of ice cream in a small bowl and spoon Chocolate Syrup (see page 212) or Ganache (see page 209) around the scoops of ice cream. Serve immediately.

TO PREPARE AHEAD: Through step 5, the base can be made the day before and refrigerated, covered. Or through step 6, ice cream will keep in the freezer for up to 1 week.

SPAGO CHOCOLATE

APRICOT ICE CREAM

Makes about 2 quarts

The richness of this ice cream may remind you of the taste of a Creamsicle. Apricot compote should be made only when apricots are in season. Do not peel the apricots, since there is a lot of flavor in the peel. When apricots are ripe, cooking time should be 8 to 10 minutes, a little longer for firmer apricots. The riper the apricots, the more flavorful the ice cream.

EQUIPMENT: 2 large nonreactive saucepans, food processor, large heatproof bowl plus slightly larger bowl, whisk, long-handled wooden spoon, large fine-mesh strainer, ladle, ice cream maker

APRICOT COMPOTE	ICE CREAM BASE
4 POUNDS RIPE APRICOTS, PITTED AND CUT INTO SLICES	2 CUPS MILK
2 CUPS GRANULATED SUGAR	2 CUPS HEAVY CREAM
	1 VANILLA BEAN, SPLIT LENGTHWISE
	8 EGG YOLKS
	1/2 CUP GRANULATED SUGAR

1. Make the compote: In a large heavy nonreactive saucepan, combine the apricots and sugar, and cook until the apricots are just tender, 8 to 10 minutes. Remove 2 cups of the fruit and syrup for the compote, and chill. Continue cooking the remainder of the apricots until very soft, about 15 minutes longer, stirring occasionally, to prevent scorching. The mixture should begin to thicken. Transfer to the workbowl of a food processor fitted with a steel blade, and process until pureed. (This may have to be done in two batches if your processor holds less than 7 cups.) Set aside.

2. Make the ice cream base: While the apricots continue to cook, in a clean large nonreactive saucepan, bring the milk, cream, and vanilla bean with its scrapings to a boil. In a large heatproof bowl, whisk the egg yolks. Gradually whisk in the sugar until thoroughly combined. Slowly whisk in half the hot milk mixture and then pour it back into the saucepan. Over low heat, stirring constantly with a long wooden spoon, cook until the mixture thickens and evenly coats the back of the spoon. Remove from the heat.

3. Immediately stir the thickened apricot puree into the base until well combined.* Let steep about 10 minutes. Strain back into the large heatproof bowl through a large fine-mesh strainer, pressing down on the apricots with a ladle to extract as much flavor as possible. Set the bowl in a slightly larger bowl filled with ice cubes and cold water to chill, stirring occasionally, about 30 minutes.

4. Freeze in an ice cream maker according to the manufacturer's directions. Scrape into a chilled container, cover with aluminum foil, and freeze. If made the night before, transfer the ice cream from the freezer to the refrigerator about 30 minutes before serving.

5. To serve, place scoops of ice cream in a chilled serving dish with the apricot compote spooned over.

TO PREPARE AHEAD: Through step 3, the base can be made the day before and refrigerated, covered. Or through step 4, the ice cream can be prepared and will keep in the freezer for 1 week.

* This will infuse the flavor of the apricots into the ice cream base. It will also help reduce the temperature of the ice cream base, avoiding a grainy texture.

BANANA-CHOCOLATE CHIP ICE CREAM

Makes about 2 quarts

This is like eating a chocolate-dipped banana without the mess. The bananas should always be ripe for better flavor.

EQUIPMENT: large saucepan, large heatproof bowl plus a slightly larger bowl, whisk, wooden spoon, large fine-mesh strainer, ice cream maker

2 CUPS CREAM

2½ CUPS MILK

8 EGG YOLKS

1 CUP GRANULATED SUGAR

1¾ POUNDS RIPE BANANAS (ABOUT
    4 MEDIUM), PUREED

2 TABLESPOONS DARK OR LIGHT RUM

1 TABLESPOON LEMON JUICE

¼ TEASPOON SALT

4 OUNCES SEMISWEET OR BITTERSWEET
    CHOCOLATE, CHOPPED FINE

1. In a large saucepan, bring to a boil the cream and 2 cups of the milk.

2. In a large heatproof bowl, whisk together the egg yolks and sugar. Whisk in half the milk mixture and then pour the mixture back into the saucepan. Cook over medium heat, stirring all the while with a wooden spoon, until the mixture thickens enough to coat the back of the spoon. Strain into a clean bowl and stir in the pureed bananas, rum, lemon juice, and salt. Stir in the remaining ½ cup milk. Set the bowl into a slightly larger bowl filled with ice cubes and water to chill, about 30 minutes.

3. Pour into an ice cream maker and freeze according to the manufacturer's directions. When the ice cream is almost ready to come out of the machine, add the chopped chocolate and let the machine churn just until the chips are distributed throughout the ice cream. Scrape into a large chilled container, cover carefully with aluminum foil, and place in the freezer.

4. If the ice cream is frozen overnight, transfer from the freezer to the refrigerator about 30 minutes before serving.

5. To serve, place one or two scoops of ice cream in a chilled bowl. Pass a bowl of warm chocolate sauce.

TO PREPARE AHEAD: Through step 3, the ice cream can be prepared and will keep frozen for 1 week.

BANANA SPLITS

Serves 6

Who doesn't have fond memories of an old-fashioned banana split? Barbara Lazaroff's father, Irv, asks for a banana split every time he comes to the restaurant. And when the owner's father asks, he gets! You can use different flavors of ice cream as we do, or you can use three scoops of your favorite flavor.

EQUIPMENT: 6 long wooden skewers, baking tray, medium heatproof bowl

5 OR 6 BANANAS
1 POUND MILK OR SEMISWEET CHOCOLATE, CUT INTO SMALL PIECES
PINEAPPLE ICE CREAM (SEE PAGE 181)
DAVID'S ORANGE-YOU-GLAD-IT'S-CHOCOLATE ICE CREAM (SEE PAGE 178)

BANANA–CHOCOLATE CHIP ICE CREAM (SEE PAGE 169)
CHOCOLATE SWIRL (SEE PAGE 211)

1. Peel and cut the bananas into twenty-four 1-inch chunks and place four chunks on each of six skewers. Arrange on a parchment-lined baking tray and place in the freezer until needed.

2. In a medium heatproof bowl set over a pan of simmering water, melt the chocolate. When almost melted, remove it from the heat and allow to melt completely.

3. Spoon the melted chocolate over the bananas, turning to coat as much of the bananas as possible. (If there is some banana showing, that's okay). When the chocolate hardens, slip the bananas off the skewers and refrigerate.

4. Assemble the banana split: Arrange one small scoop each of Pineapple, David's Orange-You-Glad-It's-Chocolate, and Banana–Chocolate Chip ice cream in a large bowl (round or oval). Place four chunks of chocolate-covered bananas around the scoops of ice cream and drizzle a little of the Chocolate Swirl over. Top with a dollop of whipped cream and sprinkle with chopped nuts, if desired. Serve immediately.

TO PREPARE AHEAD: Through step 3, make the coated bananas and refrigerate until serving time.

CHOCOLATE-ALMOND ICE CREAM CAKE

Serves 10 to 12

For birthdays or special occasions, this is an ice cream cake to end all ice cream cakes—light and creamy. The cake can be served alone or with a chocolate sauce.

EQUIPMENT: three 9-inch cake pans, long serrated knife, 9-inch springform pan, metal spatula, 9-inch cardboard round

CHOCOLATE CHIFFON CAKE (SEE PAGE 13)
2 CUPS ALMOND ICE CREAM WITH CHOCOLATE-DIPPED ALMONDS (SEE PAGE 165)

CHOCOLATE BAND (SEE PAGE 214)
DRAMBOUIE-FLAVORED CRÈME ANGLAISE (SEE PAGE 205), OR GANACHE (SEE PAGE 209)

1. Make the Chocolate Chiffon Cake, dividing the batter among three 9-inch layer pans and baking 20 to 25 minutes. Cool completely. Turn out the layers and level each layer with a serrated knife, saving the best layer for the top of the cake.

2. Make the Almond Ice Cream with Chocolate-Dipped Almonds and keep in the freezer until needed.

3. Cut out a wax-paper circle to fit the bottom of a 9-inch springform pan and arrange on the bottom of the pan. Cut out a long strip of wax paper and wrap around the inside of the springform pan, overlapping slightly. Secure with clear tape.

4. Place the first cake layer on the bottom of the springform pan, on top of the wax-paper circle. Using a metal spatula, spread half the ice cream evenly over the cake and return to the freezer for about 10 minutes to set. Place a second layer on the ice cream and spread the remaining ice cream over it. Top with the last layer and place in the freezer for 5 to 6 hours, up to overnight.

5. About 30 minutes before serving, make the Chocolate Band. Remove the cake from the freezer. Carefully release the cake from the springform pan and unwrap the wax paper wrapped around the inside of the pan. Invert the cake onto a flat surface, remove the bottom of the pan, and gently peel away the wax-paper circle. Replace with a 9-inch cardboard round and turn the cake right side up. Wrap the chocolate band around the cake (see page 214) and return it to the freezer. Remove from the freezer and refrigerate about 30 minutes before serving.

6. To serve, spoon the sauce over the surface of each dessert plate. Cut the cake into slices and set one slice in the center of each plate. Serve immediately.

TO PREPARE AHEAD: Through step 4, the cake can be made the day before serving.

CHOCOLATE TARTUFO

Makes about 10 tartufo ovals

On a trip to Italy, Judy tasted tartufo for the first time. She was transported. She described them as scoops of ice cream that seemed to melt in your mouth as you bit into them. This is our version. The consistency of this dessert is semi-frozen. At Spago, we take them out of the freezer just seconds before we serve them.

EQUIPMENT: medium heatproof bowl, grater, electric mixer with large bowl, small saucepan, rubber spatula, medium bowl

9 OUNCES BITTERSWEET CHOCOLATE	**1 CUP HEAVY CREAM**
3 EGG YOLKS	**2 TABLESPOONS CHAMBORD OR 1**
½ CUP GRANULATED SUGAR	**TABLESPOON VANILLA EXTRACT**
½ CUP WATER	**RASPBERRY COMPOTE (SEE PAGE 216)**

1. Cut 6 ounces of the chocolate into small chunks. In a medium heatproof bowl set over a pan of simmering water, melt the chocolate chunks. When almost melted, remove from the heat, stir, and let continue to melt. Keep warm.

2. Grate the remaining 3 ounces of chocolate and set aside.

3. In the large bowl of an electric mixer fitted with a whip or beaters, whip the egg yolks until thick.

4. While the egg yolks are being whipped, in a small saucepan, over high heat, bring the sugar and water to a boil until the syrup spins a thread (230 to 234 degrees). Large shiny bubbles will form and the syrup will thicken.

5. Remove the syrup from the heat and, with the mixer running on lowest speed, carefully pour the syrup into the egg yolks. (Try to avoid the beaters and sides of the bowl.) Raise the speed to medium and continue beating until the mixture is cooled and very thick. Scrape in the melted chocolate and beat until incorporated. The mixture will be stiff.

6. Gradually pour in the cream, beating at medium to high speed as needed until smooth. Stop the machine as necessary and scrape down the sides of the bowl and under the beaters with a rubber spatula. Add the Chambord and combine.

7. Pour into a medium bowl and freeze, covered, until firm enough to shape, 3 to 4 hours. Line a tray with wax paper. To shape the tartufo, scoop out the tartufo with 1 tablespoon and shape with a second tablespoon, forming a large, smooth oval (see photo). Dip the spoons into warm water occasionally, making it easier to scoop. Roll the oval in the reserved grated chocolate, covering the entire surface, and set it on the prepared tray. Repeat with the remaining tartufo mixture and grated chocolate. (If the tartufo mixture softens too much, return it to the freezer and then continue to mold when firm enough.) Freeze, covered, until firm.

8. To serve, spoon a little Raspberry Compote in the center of each dessert plate and set 1 or 2 tartufo ovals on the sauce. Serve immediately.

TO PREPARE AHEAD: Through step 7, the tartufo can be made 2 days ahead and frozen.

DAVID'S ORANGE-YOU-GLAD-IT'S-CHOCOLATE ICE CREAM

Makes about 1 1/2 quarts

Mary and I were testing recipes in Mary's home in Las Vegas when we decided to invite one of her dear friends, David Austin, for dinner. David told us that his favorite chocolate ice cream was flavored with orange. Of course, we had to try it, and the next day we came up with our version.

EQUIPMENT: zester, juicer, large and small saucepans, 2 large heatproof bowls plus a slightly larger bowl, whisk, long-handled wooden spoon, fine-mesh strainer, ice cream maker, small bowl

5 MEDIUM ORANGES, MANDARIN OR DOMESTIC	4 OUNCES BITTERSWEET CHOCOLATE, CHOPPED FINE
2 CUPS HEAVY CREAM	2 OR 3 LARGE NAVEL ORANGES, PEELED AND CUT INTO SEGMENTS
2 CUPS MILK	GRAND MARNIER
8 EGG YOLKS	
1/3 CUP GRANULATED SUGAR	
8 OUNCES BITTERSWEET CHOCOLATE, MELTED	

1. Remove the zest from the medium oranges, chop fine, and place in a large saucepan. Add the cream and milk, and bring to a boil. Turn off the heat, cover the pan, and let steep until the liquid is infused with the orange flavor, about 30 minutes.

2. Squeeze enough oranges to yield 2 cups orange juice. Pour into a small saucepan and reduce over medium heat until 1 cup remains. Set aside.

3. In a large heatproof bowl, whisk together the egg yolks and sugar. Whisk in the milk mixture and then pour back into the saucepan. Cook over medium heat, stirring all the while with a wooden spoon, until the mixture coats the back of the spoon. Stir in the melted chocolate, mix well, and strain the mixture through a fine-mesh strainer into a clean bowl. Strain the reserved orange juice into the chocolate mixture and whisk until well combined. Place the bowl in a larger bowl filled with ice cubes and water until chilled, about 30 minutes.

4. Freeze in an ice cream maker according to the manufacturer's directions. When the ice cream is almost ready to come out of the machine, add the chopped chocolate and let the machine churn until the chips are distributed throughout the ice cream. Scrape into a large chilled container, cover carefully with aluminum foil, and place in the freezer. Remove to the refrigerator about 30 minutes before serving.

5. About 1 hour before serving, place the navel orange segments in a small bowl. Pour enough Grand Marnier just to cover and let marinate.

6. To serve, place 1 or 2 scoops of ice cream in a chilled bowl and surround with the marinated orange segments.

TO PREPARE AHEAD: Through step 3, the ice cream base can be made and refrigerated covered overnight. Churn the ice cream 2 to 3 hours before serving. Or prepare through step 4; the ice cream will keep frozen up to 1 week.

MILK CHOCOLATE ICE CREAM

Makes about 1 1/2 quarts

Milk chocolate makes a lighter, smoother version for those of us who will take chocolate ice cream in any way, shape, or form.

EQUIPMENT: large nonreactive saucepan, large and medium heatproof bowls plus a slightly larger bowl, whisk, long-handled wooden spoon, large fine-mesh strainer, ice cream maker

2 CUPS MILK	**10 OUNCES MILK CHOCOLATE, BROKEN**
2 CUPS HEAVY CREAM	**OR CUT INTO SMALL PIECES**
8 EGG YOLKS	**GANACHE (SEE PAGE 209)**

1. In a large nonreactive saucepan, bring the milk and cream to a boil.

2. In a large heatproof bowl, whisk the egg yolks. Gradually pour the milk mixture into the bowl, whisking all the while. Return to the saucepan and cook, over medium heat, stirring with a wooden spoon, until the mixture coats the back of the spoon.

3. Meanwhile, in a medium heatproof bowl set over a pan of simmering water, melt the chocolate. Scrape into the heated milk mixture and whisk until well combined. Strain through a fine-mesh strainer into a clean large bowl. Place the bowl into a slightly larger bowl filled with ice cubes and cold water. Chill for about 30 minutes.

4. Freeze in an ice cream maker according to the manufacturer's directions. Scrape into a chilled container, cover with aluminum foil, and place in the freezer until needed. Remove to the refrigerator about 30 minutes before needed.

5. To serve, place one or two scoops in a small bowl. Spoon warm Ganache over and top with a little shaved chocolate. Serve immediately.

TO PREPARE AHEAD: Through step 3, the ice cream base can be made and refrigerated covered overnight. Churn the ice cream 2 to 3 hours before serving. Or prepare through step 4; the ice cream will keep frozen up to 1 week.

PINEAPPLE ICE CREAM

Makes about 1½ quarts

For our version of Banana Splits (see page 171), we combined Pineapple Ice Cream, David's Orange-You-Glad-It's-Chocolate Ice Cream with Chocolate Chips, and Banana–Chocolate Chip Ice Cream. All the flavors blend to make an unusual "split."

EQUIPMENT: medium nonreactive saucepan, large nonreactive saucepan, large heat-proof bowl plus a slightly larger bowl, whisk, wooden spoon, fine-mesh strainer, ice cream maker

2 CUPS UNSWEETENED PINEAPPLE JUICE	1 VANILLA BEAN, SPLIT LENGTHWISE
½ CUP GRANULATED SUGAR	AND SCRAPED
2 CUPS HEAVY CREAM	8 EGG YOLKS
2 CUPS MILK	

1. In a medium nonreactive saucepan, combine the pineapple juice and sugar. Reduce over medium heat until 1 cup remains. Set aside.

2. In a large nonreactive saucepan, bring to a boil the cream, milk, and vanilla bean with its scrapings. In a large heatproof bowl, whisk the egg yolks. Gradually pour the heated liquid into the bowl, whisking all the while. Return to the saucepan and cook over medium heat, stirring with a wooden spoon, until the mixture coats the back of the spoon.

3. Remove from the heat and pour in the pineapple juice, whisking to combine. Place the bowl in a slightly larger bowl filled with ice cubes and cold water. Chill for about 30 minutes.

4. Strain through a fine-mesh strainer into the bowl of an ice cream maker and freeze according to the manufacturer's directions. Transfer to a clean chilled container, cover with aluminum foil, and place in the freezer until needed.

TO PREPARE AHEAD: Through step 3, refrigerate, covered, overnight, churning 2 to 3 hours before serving. Or prepare through step 4. Remove the ice cream from the freezer and place in the refrigerator about 30 minutes before serving. The ice cream will keep frozen up to 1 week.

CRUNCHY TOFFEE TORTONI

EQUIPMENT: 2 medium bowls, whisk or egg beater, small heavy saucepan, rubber spatula, eight ¾-cup ramekins, tray for the ramekins

1 CUP HEAVY CREAM	**3 EGG YOLKS**
	2 TABLESPOONS AMARETTO
SUGAR SYRUP	**½ TEASPOON ALMOND EXTRACT**
⅓ CUP GRANULATED SUGAR	**½ CUP FINELY CHOPPED CHOCOLATE-**
2 TABLESPOONS COLD WATER	**ALMOND TOFFEE (SEE PAGE 131)**
1 VANILLA BEAN, SPLIT LENGTHWISE	**CHOCOLATE CURLS (SEE PAGE 213)**
AND SCRAPED	**FOR TOPPING**

1. In a medium bowl, using a whisk or egg beaters, whip the cream until it holds soft peaks. Cover and refrigerate until needed.

2. Make the Sugar Syrup: In a small heavy saucepan, combine the sugar, water, and vanilla bean with its scrapings. Over medium heat, bring to a boil and continue to boil for 3 minutes.

3. Meanwhile, in another medium bowl, whip the egg yolks. Whisk in the Amaretto. Gradually whisk in the boiling Sugar Syrup and then set aside until cool to the touch.

4. Stir a little of the whipped cream into the yolk mixture and then, with a rubber spatula, fold back into the whipped cream until well incorporated. Fold in ¼ cup of the chopped toffee.

5. Spoon into eight ¾-cup ramekins and sprinkle the remaining toffee over the tops. Set the ramekins on a tray (this will make handling easier and will keep the tortoni level) and place in the freezer for at least 3 to 4 hours, up to overnight. If freezing overnight, cover with plastic wrap.

6. To serve, arrange a few chocolate curls on top of each portion and place the tortoni ramekin on a small doily-lined dessert plate. Pass a plate of cookies.

TO PREPARE AHEAD: Through step 5, the tortoni can be made 1 day ahead.

TÍA MARÍA–COFFEE ICE CREAM WITH FUDGE SWIRL

Makes about 1 1/2 quarts

Mark Ferguson, chef of Lupo, our newest restaurant in Las Vegas, provided us with his grandfather's recipe. The taste brings back fond memories of his youth. Spago customers love it, too.

EQUIPMENT: small saucepan, 2 or 3 large heatproof bowls plus a slightly larger bowl, large fine-mesh strainer, rolling pin, large nonreactive saucepan, whisk, wooden spoon, ice cream maker

FUDGE SWIRL	ICE CREAM
2 CUPS SUGAR SYRUP (SEE PAGE 217)	1/2 CUP DECAFFEINATED ESPRESSO BEANS
6 OUNCES BITTERSWEET CHOCOLATE,	2 CUPS MILK
CUT INTO SMALL PIECES	2 CUPS HEAVY CREAM
1 CUP UNSWEETENED COCOA POWDER	8 EGG YOLKS
1 TEASPOON VANILLA EXTRACT	1/2 CUP GRANULATED SUGAR
	1/2 CUP TÍA MARÍA

1. Make the Fudge Swirl: In a small saucepan, bring the Sugar Syrup to a boil. In a large heatproof bowl, combine the chocolate and cocoa and pour the Sugar Syrup over. Place the bowl over a pan of simmering water and stir to combine. When the chocolate has almost melted, remove from the heat and let continue to melt, stirring occasionally. Stir in the vanilla and strain into a clean bowl. Let cool and then refrigerate, covered, until needed.

2. Make the ice cream: Place the espresso beans in a small plastic bag. Secure the bag and gently roll a rolling pin over the bag, crushing the beans. Set aside.

3. In a large nonreactive saucepan, bring the milk and cream to a boil. Remove from the heat, add the crushed beans, and stir to combine. Cover the pan with foil or a lid and let steep until the desired flavor is reached, about 30 minutes, or longer if you like a stronger coffee flavor.

4. In a large heatproof bowl, whisk together the egg yolks and sugar. Bring the coffee mixture back to a boil and gradually pour into the egg yolk mixture, whisking all the while. Return the mixture to the saucepan and cook over low to medium heat, stirring with a wooden spoon, until the mixture coats the back of the spoon. (Lift the spoon from the pan and run your finger down the back of the spoon. If it leaves a narrow furrow, the mixture is ready.)

5. Strain into a large clean bowl and stir in the Tía María. Place the bowl in a slightly larger bowl filled with ice cubes and water. Chill for about 30 minutes.

6. Freeze in an ice cream maker according to the manufacturer's directions. Scrape into a chilled container and swirl some of the Fudge Swirl through, reserving 1 cup for later use. Cover with aluminum foil and place in the freezer until needed.

7. To serve, place 1 or 2 scoops in a small bowl. Warm the reserved sauce and spoon a little of the sauce over. Serve immediately. Mark prefers to crush some of the coffee beans, sprinkle a little over the ice cream, and top with a splash of Tía María.

TO PREPARE AHEAD: Through step 5, refrigerate, covered, overnight. Continue with the recipe the next day. Or prepare through step 6, placing the container in the refrigerator about 30 minutes before serving. The ice cream will keep frozen up to 1 week.

VANILLA LOW-FAT YOGURT

Makes about 4 cups

This is the base for our Low-Fat Frozen Chocolate Yogurt (see page 188). Yogurt starter can be purchased in a health food store. After you make your first batch of yogurt, remove 2 tablespoons before combining it with chocolate or fruit puree and keep this as a starter for your next batch of yogurt. To make fruit yogurt, combine 4 cups vanilla yogurt with 1 cup granulated sugar and about 2 cups of fruit puree. You can use strawberries, raspberries, bananas, or other fruit. Whole milk can be substituted for low-fat milk.

EQUIPMENT: large nonreactive saucepan, flame tamer, candy thermometer, large bowl, pan large enough to hold bowl

4 CUPS LOW-FAT MILK

**1 VANILLA BEAN, SPLIT LENGTHWISE
AND SCRAPED**

2 TABLESPOONS YOGURT STARTER

1. In a large nonreactive saucepan, combine the milk and vanilla bean with its scrapings. Place the pan over a flame tamer* to prevent scorching the milk and attach a stainless-steel candy thermometer to the rim of the inside of the pan. (The thermometer should not touch the bottom of the pan.)

2. Over very low heat, bring the milk temperature to 180 degrees. Continue cooking, maintaining the 180-degree temperature for 30 minutes, lowering or raising the heat slightly as necessary. Watch carefully so that the milk does not boil over. Turn off the heat and cool to 105 degrees. (You can set the pan over cold water to cool more quickly.)

3. Spoon the yogurt starter into a large bowl, add a little of the cooled milk, and stir to make a paste. Gradually pour in a little more milk, stirring, until the powder is completely dissolved. Pour back into the saucepan, stir to combine thoroughly, then return to the bowl and cover with foil. If using an electric oven, place the bowl in a pan and pour enough tepid water into the pan to reach about 1 inch up the sides of the bowl. Transfer to the rack in the oven for 8 to 10 hours, up to overnight. If using a

---

* A flame tamer is a round perforated metal disk. It has a wooden handle attached for easy handling. Setting the pan on the disk allows the liquid to heat more slowly and helps prevent scorching.

gas oven, the water bath is not necessary. Just cover the bowl and place it on the top shelf of the oven. The yogurt is ready when thickened.

4. Carefully remove the bowl from the oven and take out 2 tablespoons of yogurt to use as a starter for the next batch. Refrigerate until needed.

TO PREPARE AHEAD: Through step 4, yogurt can be made and will keep in the refrigerator for up to 5 days.

LOW-FAT FROZEN CHOCOLATE YOGURT

Makes about 1½ quarts

Caramel Sauce (see page 206), dried cherries that have marinated in juice of your choice, or coarsely chopped toasted nuts can be folded into the yogurt before freezing, if desired.

EQUIPMENT: large bowl, ice cream maker

1 QUART VANILLA LOW-FAT YOGURT (SEE PAGE 186), WELL CHILLED

1 CUP CHOCOLATE SYRUP (SEE PAGE 212)

½ CUP LIGHT CORN SYRUP

¼ TEASPOON SALT

1. In a large bowl, combine all the ingredients and mix well, adding more chocolate syrup, if desired, to taste. Freeze in an ice cream maker according to the manufacturer's directions. Transfer to a container, cover well, and freeze.

2. To serve, arrange 1 or 2 scoops of yogurt in a chilled serving dish and surround with orange segments that have been marinated in Grand Marnier, if desired.

TO PREPARE AHEAD: Through step 1, the yogurt can be made and frozen for up to 5 days.

FILLINGS AND SAUCES

*N*o dessert is complete until you add the finishing touch. It can be something as simple as confectioners' sugar sifted over the top of a cake, on the plate, or both. Presentation is almost as important as the dessert itself. Your eyes tell you if you want to try a dessert; your taste validates your decision.

With that in mind, we have included a variety of fillings and sauces that are interchangeable and will complement many of the desserts in the book. We have suggested how best to use each of the recipes, but the choice is yours.

For example, the Chocolate Band (see page 214) can be wrapped around almost any cake, white or chocolate. A mousse can be piped between cake layers, served in a goblet with fruit, or spooned into the center of a cake after it has been unmolded from a tube pan.

Many of the recipes can be prepared ahead, some as far as two weeks in advance; the Sugar Syrup can be refrigerated indefinitely. This should prove to be very helpful when planning a menu because we all appreciate how precious time is.

. . .

CHOCOLATE BUTTERCREAM

Makes enough to fill and frost two
9-inch layers

This is our favorite way to frost a cake. Unlike a mousse, buttercream can be refrigerated, covered, for up to 2 weeks, which makes it easy to frost a cake at your convenience.

EQUIPMENT: medium heatproof bowl, electric mixer with 2 or 3 large bowls, 2-quart nonreactive saucepan, long-handled wooden spoon, rubber spatula, fine-mesh strainer

6 OUNCES BITTERSWEET CHOCOLATE, CUT INTO SMALL PIECES

7 EGG YOLKS

2/3 CUP GRANULATED SUGAR

1/2 CUP MILK

1 TABLESPOON UNSWEETENED COCOA POWDER

1 POUND (4 STICKS) UNSALTED BUTTER, AT ROOM TEMPERATURE, CUT INTO SMALL PIECES

1. In a medium heatproof bowl set over a pan of simmering water, melt the chocolate. When almost melted, turn off the heat and allow to melt completely, stirring occasionally.

2. In the large bowl of an electric mixer fitted with a paddle or beaters, beat the egg yolks with 3 tablespoons of the sugar until the mixture is thick and pale yellow and forms a ribbon when the beaters are lifted, 4 to 5 minutes.

3. Meanwhile, in a 2-quart nonreactive saucepan, bring the milk just to a boil. Using a long-handled wooden spoon, stir in the melted chocolate, cocoa, and remaining sugar until completely dissolved.

4. With the mixer running on its lowest speed, slowly pour about one-third of the milk mixture into the yolks. Turn off the machine and use a rubber spatula to scrape the mixture back into the saucepan. Cook over medium heat, stirring frequently, until you see the first bubbles. Immediately remove from the heat and quickly strain through a fine-mesh strainer into a clean large bowl of the mixer. Beat on medium-high speed until thick and the bottom of the bowl is completely cool to the touch. Set aside.

5. In another clean bowl of the mixer, using clean paddle or beaters, on medium speed, beat the butter until it begins to whiten and is very fluffy. On low speed, slowly pour

the milk mixture into the butter. At first, as you pour, the mixture appears broken, but it will come back together as the speed is increased. When all the milk mixture has been poured, gradually increase the speed and beat until it looks like whipped butter. It is now ready and can be used immediately if desired.

TO PREPARE AHEAD: Through step 5, the buttercream can be refrigerated, covered for up to 2 weeks.

CHOCOLATE PASTRY CREAM

Makes about 3 cups

This is a versatile filling for napoleons, pastries, tarts, or cakes. To make Mocha Pastry Cream, add ¼ cup crushed* coffee beans (regular or decaffeinated) to the scalded milk in step 1 below and let it steep for 15 minutes. Strain and continue with the recipe.

EQUIPMENT: medium saucepan, small heatproof bowl, electric mixer with large bowl, long-handled wooden spoon, large fine-mesh strainer, medium bowl, whisk

2 CUPS MILK

4 OUNCES BITTERSWEET CHOCOLATE,
   CUT INTO VERY SMALL PIECES

4 EGG YOLKS

½ CUP GRANULATED SUGAR

3 TABLESPOONS ALL-PURPOSE FLOUR,
   SIFTED

1. In a medium saucepan, scald the milk.

2. In a small heatproof bowl set over simmering water, melt the chocolate. When almost melted, turn off the heat and let melt completely, stirring occasionally.

3. Meanwhile, in the large bowl of an electric mixer fitted with a paddle or beaters, on high speed beat the egg yolks and sugar until the mixture is pale yellow and forms a ribbon when the beaters are lifted from the bowl. (If you have a strong arm, this can also be done with a whisk and large mixing bowl.) Whisk in the flour.

4. Turn the speed to low and slowly pour about one-third of the milk into the yolk mixture. Mix until combined. Pour the contents back into the saucepan and cook over medium heat, stirring constantly with a wooden spoon, until the mixture thickens and bubbles begin to appear on the surface. *Immediately* pour through a fine-mesh strainer into a clean medium bowl and whisk in the melted chocolate. Cover with plastic wrap placed directly on the surface of the cream to prevent a skin forming. Refrigerate and use as desired.

TO PREPARE AHEAD: Through step 4, the pastry cream can be made and refrigerated for up to 3 days.

*To crush coffee beans, place in a plastic bag, close the bag, and heavily press a rolling pin over the beans.

VANILLA PASTRY CREAM

Makes about 3 cups

Anyone who has ever worked in a pastry kitchen knows that Vanilla Pastry Cream comes under the heading of Lesson Number 1. Once you have mastered pastry cream, you can make any number of desserts using it—simple fruit tarts with pastry cream spread on the bottom crust, as a filling for a cake, or as a custard, spooned over fresh fruit.

EQUIPMENT: medium nonreactive saucepan, electric mixer with large bowl, whisk, long-handled wooden spoon, fine-mesh strainer, medium bowl

2 CUPS MILK

1 VANILLA BEAN, SPLIT LENGTHWISE
   AND SCRAPED

6 EGG YOLKS

½ CUP GRANULATED SUGAR

3 TABLESPOONS ALL-PURPOSE FLOUR,
   SIFTED

1. In a medium nonreactive saucepan, scald the milk with the vanilla bean and its scrapings.

2. While the milk is being scalded, in the large bowl of an electric mixer fitted with a paddle or beaters, on high speed beat the egg yolks and sugar until the mixture is pale yellow and forms a ribbon when the beaters are lifted from the bowl. (This also can be done with a whisk and large mixing bowl, if desired.) Whisk in the flour.

3. Turn the speed to low and pour about half the hot milk into the egg yolk mixture. Turn off the mixer, pour the contents back into the saucepan, and cook over medium heat, stirring constantly with a wooden spoon, until the mixture thickens and bubbles begin to appear on the surface. *Immediately* pour through a fine-mesh strainer into a clean medium bowl and cover with plastic wrap placed directly on the surface of the cream to prevent a skin forming on top. Refrigerate overnight and use as desired.

TO PREPARE AHEAD: Through step 3, pastry cream can be made and refrigerated for up to 3 days.

CHOCOLATE MOUSSE

Makes about 7 cups

Though it's commonly known as mousse, at Spago we call this versatile dessert a chocolate charlotte. Regardless of the title, it's delicious. After the mousse sets up, it can be used as a filling for a layer cake or for our crêpes. Or if you prefer, spoon it into champagne glasses over fresh raspberries.

EQUIPMENT: medium and large heatproof bowls, electric mixer with 2 large bowls, small saucepan, whisk, rubber spatula

12 OUNCES BITTERSWEET CHOCOLATE, CUT INTO SMALL PIECES	**6 EGG YOLKS**
3 CUPS HEAVY CREAM	**¾ CUP GRANULATED SUGAR**
	½ CUP WATER

1. In a medium heatproof bowl set over a pan of simmering water, melt the chocolate. When almost melted, turn off the heat and let the chocolate continue to melt completely, stirring occasionally. Keep the bowl over the warm water until ready to use.

2. Meanwhile, in the large bowl of an electric mixer fitted with a whip or beaters, whip the cream until soft peaks form. Refrigerate, covered, until needed.

3. Place the egg yolks in a large heatproof bowl and set aside.

4. In a small saucepan, combine the sugar and water, and bring to a boil. Boil until the sugar dissolves, about 3 minutes, making sugar syrup. Whisking constantly, pour the boiling syrup over the egg yolks. Set the bowl over a pan of simmering water and immediately start to whisk, whisking until the mixture is thick and white in color. The mixture should be hot to the touch.

5. Remove the bowl from the heat and, working quickly, scrape the egg mixture into another clean large bowl of the electric mixer. On medium-high speed, using whip or beaters, beat until the volume has doubled and the bottom of the bowl is completely cool to the touch. Turn the speed to low, scrape in the warm melted chocolate, and continue to beat until well combined. Remove the bowl from the mixer, and using a rubber spatula, very carefully and gently fold in half the whipped cream. Then fold in the remaining cream. The mixture should resemble softly whipped

cream. This can be used immediately or refrigerated, covered, until needed. If the mixture seems a little runny, the chocolate may have been too warm, but after refrigerating for an hour or so, it will be fine.

TO PREPARE AHEAD: Through step 5, the mousse can be made 1 day ahead and refrigerated, covered. Remove about 15 minutes before needed and whisk vigorously with a wire whip for 1 minute to restore its original texture.

CHOCOLATE-HAZELNUT MOUSSE

Makes 4 cups

Chocolate-Hazelnut Mousse is an elegant variation on Chocolate Mousse with hazelnut paste. Like Chocolate Mousse, this can be spooned into attractive goblets, topped with a bit of whipped cream, and served as is, or used as a filling for a layer cake. It also can be piped over the cooled Hazelnut Brownies (see page 52), creating a simple but surprisingly memorable dessert.

EQUIPMENT: small baking tray, clean towel, food processor, large bowl, whisk or eggbeater, 2 medium heatproof bowls, small saucepan, electric mixer with large bowl, rubber spatula

5 OUNCES UNBLANCHED HAZELNUTS	**3 EGG YOLKS**
1 TABLESPOON PLUS ½ TEASPOON	**⅓ CUP GRANULATED SUGAR**
HAZELNUT OIL*	**¼ CUP WATER**
1½ CUPS HEAVY CREAM	
5 OUNCES MILK CHOCOLATE, CUT INTO	
SMALL PIECES	

1. Position the rack in the center of the oven and preheat the oven to 350 degrees. Arrange the hazelnuts on a small baking tray and bake until lightly browned, 10 to 12 minutes, turning the tray back to front after 5 or 6 minutes. Cool. Enclose the nuts in a clean towel and rub until as much of the skins as possible comes off.

2. Place the nuts and hazelnut oil in the workbowl of a food processor fitted with a steel blade and process until a paste forms.

3. Meanwhile, in a large bowl, using a whisk or eggbeater, whip the heavy cream. Refrigerate, covered, until needed.

4. In a medium heatproof bowl set over a pan of simmering water, melt the chocolate. Turn off the heat when almost melted and stir occasionally until completely melted. Scrape into the nut paste and process until thoroughly mixed. Set aside.

5. In a clean medium heatproof bowl, lightly whisk the egg yolks.

* If hazelnut oil is not available, peanut or safflower oil can be substituted.

6. In a small saucepan, bring to a boil the sugar and water, and continue to boil until the sugar dissolves, about 3 minutes. Whisk the boiling syrup into the egg yolks and set the bowl over a saucepan of simmering water. Continue to whisk until the mixture is thick, pale yellow, and hot to the touch.

7. Remove from the heat and scrape into the large bowl of an electric mixer fitted with a paddle or beaters. On medium-high speed, beat until the mixture has doubled in volume and the bottom of the bowl is completely cool to the touch. Turn the speed to low, scrape the hazelnut paste into the bowl, and continue to beat until well combined.

8. Remove the bowl from the mixer and with a rubber spatula, very carefully and gently fold in half the whipped cream, then the remaining half. The mixture should resemble softly whipped cream. Refrigerate, covered, and use as needed as filling or frosting.

TO PREPARE AHEAD: Through step 8, the mousse can be made 1 day ahead and refrigerated, covered. Remove about 15 minutes before needed and whisk vigorously with a wire whip for 1 minute to restore its original texture.

MOCHA MOUSSE

Makes about 4 cups

Mocha Mousse has the same flavor as a really rich mochaccino, a cappuccino with cocoa. Like Chocolate Mousse, this can be used as a filling or frosting for a layer cake. It also can be spooned into tall goblets, served with or without whipped cream.

EQUIPMENT: large bowl, whisk or eggbeater, 2 medium heatproof bowls, small saucepan, electric mixer with large bowl, rubber spatula

2 CUPS HEAVY CREAM	**⅓ CUP WATER**
8 OUNCES BITTERSWEET CHOCOLATE,	**1 TABLESPOON PLUS 1 TEASPOON**
CUT INTO SMALL PIECES	**INSTANT ESPRESSO**
⅓ CUP GRANULATED SUGAR	**4 EGG YOLKS**

1. In a large bowl, using a whisk or eggbeater, whip the heavy cream. Refrigerate, covered, until needed.

2. In a medium heatproof bowl set over a pan of simmering water, melt the chocolate. When almost melted, turn off the heat and stir occasionally until completely melted. Set aside.

3. In a small saucepan, bring to a boil the sugar and water, and boil until the sugar dissolves, about 3 minutes. Whisk the instant espresso into the boiling syrup to dilute.

4. Place the egg yolks in a clean medium heatproof bowl. Whisk the boiling syrup into the egg yolks. Set the bowl over simmering water and continue to whisk until the mixture is thick and hot to the touch.

5. Remove from the heat and scrape into the large bowl of an electric mixer fitted with a paddle or beaters. On medium-high speed, beat until the mixture has doubled in volume and the bottom of the bowl is completely cool to the touch. Turn the speed to low, scrape the chocolate into the bowl, and continue to beat until well combined.

6. Remove the bowl from the mixer and using a rubber spatula, very carefully and gently fold in half the whipped cream, then the remaining half. The mixture should resemble softly whipped cream. Refrigerate, covered, until needed.

TO PREPARE AHEAD: Through step 6, the mousse can be made 1 day ahead and re-frigerated, covered. Remove about 15 minutes before needed and whisk vigorously with a wire whip for 1 minute to restore its original texture.

WHITE CHOCOLATE MOUSSE

Because white chocolate has a subtle flavor, this mousse can be used as a sophisticated whipped cream. Layer the mousse with sliced strawberries, blueberries, or a combination of the two, and you have an elegant dessert.

EQUIPMENT: large bowl, whisk or eggbeater, large heatproof bowl, rubber spatula

1½ CUPS PLUS 3 TABLESPOONS HEAVY CREAM

8 OUNCES WHITE CHOCOLATE, CUT INTO SMALL PIECES

1 TABLESPOON FRESH LEMON JUICE

1. In a large bowl, using a whisk or eggbeater, whip 1½ cups of the cream until stiff peaks form. Refrigerate, covered, until needed.

2. In a large heatproof bowl set over a pan of simmering water, melt the chocolate with the lemon juice and the remaining 3 tablespoons of cream. When almost melted, turn off the heat and allow to melt completely, stirring occasionally. Cool.

3. Whisk one-quarter of the whipped cream into the white chocolate mixture, then with a rubber spatula very carefully and gently fold back into the whipped cream.

4. To serve, pipe or spoon as needed.

TO PREPARE AHEAD: Through step 3, the mousse can be made 1 day ahead and refrigerated, covered. Remove about 15 minutes before needed and whisk vigorously with a wire whip for 1 minute to restore its original texture.

RICOTTA FILLING

This filling can be used for Six-Layer Cassata (page 7). We have substituted dried cherries for the candied fruit usually found in ricotta-filled pastries. If desired, you can combine 1 cup ricotta with ½ cup mascarpone cheese and continue with the recipe.

EQUIPMENT: food processor, small bowl

16 OUNCES WHOLE-MILK OR LOW-FAT
RICOTTA CHEESE

¾ CUP GRANULATED SUGAR

1 CUP DRIED SOUR CHERRIES

2 TABLESPOONS GRATED ORANGE ZEST

3 OUNCES COARSELY GRATED MILK
CHOCOLATE

1. In the workbowl of a food processor fitted with a steel blade, combine the ricotta, sugar, cherries, and orange zest. Process until well chopped.

2. Add the chocolate and combine with a few on/off turns.

3. Scrape into a small bowl and refrigerate, covered, 2 to 3 hours, up to overnight.

TO PREPARE AHEAD: Through step 3, the filling can be made the day before serving.

TOASTED ALMOND PASTRY CREAM

Makes about 3 cups

The toasted almond gives this pastry cream a distinct flavor. It is absolutely wonderful spooned into Chocolate Crêpes (see page 66), the crêpes dusted with sifted confectioners' sugar—or as a tart filling or cake frosting. Use your imagination!

EQUIPMENT: electric mixer with large bowl, whisk, medium saucepan, long-handled wooden spoon, large fine-mesh strainer, medium bowl

2 OUNCES (ABOUT ½ CUP) WHOLE ALMONDS, TOASTED (SEE PAGE 165, STEPS 1 AND 2)	3 TABLESPOONS ALL-PURPOSE FLOUR, SIFTED
8 EGG YOLKS	1 TEASPOON ALMOND EXTRACT
½ CUP GRANULATED SUGAR	2⅔ CUPS WHOLE MILK

1. Chop the toasted almonds fine and set aside.

2. In the large bowl of an electric mixer fitted with a paddle or beaters, beat the egg yolks and sugar on high speed until the mixture is pale yellow and forms a ribbon when the beaters are lifted from the bowl. (This also can be done with a whisk and large bowl.) Whisk in the flour and almond extract until smooth.

3. Meanwhile, in a medium saucepan, over medium heat, scald the milk. Turn the mixer speed to low and slowly pour about half the milk into the egg mixture. Pour back into the saucepan and cook over medium heat, stirring constantly with a wooden spoon, until the mixture thickens and bubbles just *begin* to appear on the surface. *Immediately* pour through a fine-mesh strainer into a clean medium bowl, fold in the reserved almonds, and cover with plastic wrap placed directly on the cream to prevent a skin forming on top. Refrigerate overnight and use as needed.

TO PREPARE AHEAD: Through step 3, the pastry cream can be made and refrigerated for up to 3 days.

GRAND MARNIER SAUCE

This sauce can be spooned over ice cream, to accompany chocolate cake or chocolate crêpes, as well as for the White Chocolate Soufflé (see page 141).

EQUIPMENT: medium heavy saucepan

2 CUPS ORANGE JUICE	**1 CUP GRANULATED SUGAR**
1 CUP GRAND MARNIER, TRIPLE SEC, OR	
OTHER ORANGE-FLAVORED LIQUEUR	

1. In a medium heavy saucepan, combine all the ingredients. Over medium-high heat, bring to a boil and continue to heat until 1¾ cups remain, stirring occasionally. The sauce thickens slightly as it cooks and foam will form on top, but that will subside.

2. Serve warm or at room temperature.

TO PREPARE AHEAD: Through step 1, the sauce can be made 1 day ahead and does not need to be refrigerated. Just keep covered. If serving warm, reheat over low heat.

DRAMBUIE-FLAVORED CRÈME ANGLAISE

Makes about 2 1/2 cups

This versatile sauce can accompany any number of desserts, such as Crunchy Toffee Tortoni or Buttermilk Layer Cake. If you prefer, the sauce can be flavored with chocolate, mocha, orange, or liqueur of your choice. It can be infused with crushed coffee beans, or praline can be folded into it.

EQUIPMENT: 2 medium bowls, whisk, medium saucepan, long-handled wooden spoon, large fine-mesh strainer, large bowl, larger bowl

4 EGG YOLKS	**1 VANILLA BEAN, SPLIT LENGTHWISE**
3 TABLESPOONS GRANULATED SUGAR	**AND SCRAPED**
2 CUPS HEAVY CREAM	**3 TABLESPOONS DRAMBUIE, OR**
1 1/2 TABLESPOONS SOUR CREAM	**TO TASTE**

1. In a medium bowl, whisk together the egg yolks and sugar until very pale yellow and smooth.

2. In a medium saucepan, bring to a boil the heavy cream, sour cream, and vanilla bean with its scrapings. Whisk about half this mixture into the egg yolk mixture until well combined, then pour back into the saucepan. Over medium heat, stirring constantly with a wooden spoon, cook until the mixture coats the back of the spoon. (It is very important to stir constantly. Do not overcook; cooking too long will result in scrambled eggs.)

3. Pour through a fine-mesh strainer into a clean bowl and immediately set the bowl over a larger bowl filled with ice cubes and cold water until chilled, stirring occasionally, about 30 minutes. Stir in the liqueur. Refrigerate, covered, until needed.

TO PREPARE AHEAD: Through step 3, the crème anglaise can be made up to 3 days ahead.

CARAMEL SAUCE

Makes 2 cups

You will find Caramel Sauce a very convenient item to have in your refrigerator. When needed, reheat over a pan of simmering water until pourable, and spoon over ice cream or frozen yogurt. Pour it into a squeeze bottle and use it to decorate your dessert plates for a spectacular professional look. It also can be used cold as a swirl for ice cream (see Chocolate Swirl, page 211).

EQUIPMENT: deep medium heavy saucepan, long-handled wooden spoon, large fine-mesh strainer, medium heatproof bowl

1¼ CUPS GRANULATED SUGAR

½ CUP WATER

1½ CUPS HEAVY CREAM, HEATED

1½ OUNCES (3 TABLESPOONS) UNSALTED BUTTER, AT ROOM TEMPERATURE, CUT INTO SMALL PIECES

1. In a deep medium heavy saucepan, combine the sugar and water, and cook, over moderate heat, until the mixture becomes golden brown, 15 to 20 minutes. After 10 minutes, watch carefully to prevent burning.

2. Remove the saucepan from the heat and immediately pour in the heated cream, stirring with a long-handled wooden spoon until smooth. Use an oven mitt while stirring because the sauce will bubble up and the steam is extremely hot.

3. Sprinkle the butter into the sauce and allow to melt, then stir to combine thoroughly. Strain through a fine-mesh strainer into a clean medium heatproof bowl. Use as needed.

TO PREPARE AHEAD: Through step 3, the sauce can be refrigerated, covered, and will keep 2 or 3 weeks.

ORANGE-CARAMEL SAUCE

Makes about 1¼ cups

This delicate sauce can be served warm over ice cream or ice cream cake. You might also try it with our Classic Chocolate Soufflé (see page 137).

EQUIPMENT: small nonreactive saucepan, fine-mesh strainer, pastry brush

ZEST OF 4 MEDIUM ORANGES, CHOPPED FINE	**¼ CUP WATER**
	½ CUP ORANGE JUICE
½ CUP GRANULATED SUGAR	**½ CUP GRAND MARNIER**

1. In a small nonreactive saucepan, combine the orange zest with water to cover, bring to a boil, and boil for 1 minute. Strain through a fine-mesh strainer, remove the orange zest, and set aside.

2. In the same pan, bring the sugar and water to a boil. Do not stir or whisk, but if crystals form around the sides of the pan, brush down with a pastry brush that has been dipped in cold water. Over medium heat, cook to a dark caramel color, about 15 minutes. Watch carefully the last few minutes to prevent the syrup from burning.

3. Remove from the heat and add the reserved orange zest, orange juice, and Grand Marnier. Set over low heat and stir until smooth, about 2 minutes.

4. Serve warm or at room temperature, making certain that a little of the zest is spooned over with each serving.

TO PREPARE AHEAD: Through step 3, the sauce can be prepared and will keep 3 or 4 days refrigerated. Reheat over low heat.

CHOCOLATE FROSTING

To frost one 8- or 9-inch layer cake

Makes about 2¼ cups

This super dark and creamy frosting can be used for layer cakes as well as cookie fillings. It can be easily doubled or tripled.

EQUIPMENT: 2 medium heatproof bowls, electric mixer with large bowl, rubber spatula, small saucepan

12 OUNCES BITTERSWEET CHOCOLATE, CUT INTO SMALL PIECES *+ used ½ g.*	½ CUP CONFECTIONERS' SUGAR
8 OUNCES (2 STICKS) UNSALTED BUTTER, AT ROOM TEMPERATURE, CUT INTO SMALL PIECES	¾ CUP UNSWEETENED COCOA POWDER
	½ CUP STRONG COFFEE OR WATER

+ used ¾ but 7 ½ c. is nec.

1. In a medium heatproof bowl set over a pan of simmering water, melt the chocolate. When almost melted, turn off the heat and allow to melt completely, stirring occasionally.

2. While the chocolate is melting, in the large bowl of an electric mixer fitted with a paddle or beaters, beat the butter and sugar until fluffy, stopping the mixer occasionally and scraping down the sides of the bowl and under the beaters as necessary with a rubber spatula. Start on slow speed and, when combined, turn up the speed to high.

3. In a small saucepan, over low heat, dissolve the cocoa in the coffee, stirring as necessary. Remove from the heat, scrape the melted chocolate into the saucepan, and stir to combine thoroughly. On low speed, pour into the butter-sugar mixture, again stopping the mixer and scraping down the sides of the bowl and under the beaters. Beat until smooth and shiny. Transfer to a medium bowl and set aside until of spreading consistency. Use as needed.

TO PREPARE AHEAD: Through step 3, frosting can be prepared 1 day ahead. Refrigerate, covered, until needed.

GANACHE

Ganache can be spread over a cake layer as a frosting, or used as a sauce. The Ganache will thicken as it chills, but it can be brought back to the proper consistency either by leaving at room temperature or setting over a pan of simmering water. Untoasted pecans, toasted unblanched almonds, or hazelnuts can be chopped and folded into the ganache. (Hazelnuts need to be peeled after toasting, then chopped.) If desired, finely chopped orange zest or vanilla extract can be added to flavor the Ganache.

EQUIPMENT: medium heatproof bowl, small saucepan, whisk

3/4 POUND BITTERSWEET OR SEMISWEET CHOCOLATE, CUT INTO SMALL PIECES

1 CUP HEAVY CREAM

1. Place the chocolate in a medium heatproof bowl and set aside.

2. In a small saucepan, bring the cream to a boil. Pour over the chocolate, let sit for 2 or 3 minutes, then whisk until smooth and shiny. Cool slightly and add about 1/2 cup chopped nuts, if desired. Refrigerate, covered.

3. Use as needed.

TO PREPARE AHEAD: Through step 2, Ganache can be made as much as 1 to 2 weeks ahead and refrigerated.

CHOCOLATE GLAZE

A glaze differs from a frosting in that it is poured over a cake. It has a shiny glossiness when it sets. A glaze has many uses. Before frosting a cake that's not completely smooth, we pour the glaze over, let it set, and then frost. The frosting then will be much smoother and give the cake a more professional look. When the glaze becomes slightly firm, it also can be rolled into small truffles or piped between two cookies as a filling.

EQUIPMENT: 2 medium heatproof bowls, whisk, fine-mesh strainer

8 OUNCES BITTERSWEET CHOCOLATE, CUT INTO SMALL PIECES

3 OUNCES (¾ STICK) UNSALTED BUTTER, CUT INTO SMALL PIECES

⅓ CUP LIGHT CORN SYRUP

⅓ CUP BRANDY

1. In a medium heatproof bowl, combine the chocolate and butter and set over a pan of simmering water. Do not let the bottom of the bowl touch the water or the chocolate may burn. Let melt almost completely, turn off the heat, and let the mixture continue to melt, stirring occasionally.

2. Whisk in the corn syrup and brandy until smooth. Pour through a fine-mesh strainer into a clean medium bowl and reserve, covered, in a warm spot until needed.

TO PREPARE AHEAD: Through step 2, the glaze can be made 2 or 3 days ahead, refrigerated, covered, and remelted over simmering water when needed. Let sit over the warm water until smooth, stirring occasionally.

CHOCOLATE SWIRL

Makes 2 1/2 cups

As the name implies, this sauce either can be swirled through ice cream when it is almost ready to come out of the ice cream maker or it can be spooned over finished ice cream.

EQUIPMENT: 2 medium heatproof bowls, medium saucepan, whisk, fine-mesh strainer

1 CUP UNSWEETENED COCOA POWDER	1 TEASPOON VANILLA EXTRACT
6 OUNCES BITTERSWEET CHOCOLATE,	2 1/2 CUPS WATER
CUT INTO SMALL PIECES	2 CUPS GRANULATED SUGAR

1. In a medium heatproof bowl, combine the cocoa, chocolate, and vanilla. Set aside.

2. In a medium saucepan, bring the water and sugar to a boil and continue to boil until the sugar has completely dissolved, about 5 minutes. Pour into the chocolate mixture and whisk until smooth.

3. Strain through a fine-mesh strainer into a clean medium heatproof bowl and use as needed.

TO PREPARE AHEAD: Through step 3, the swirl can be made and will keep for up to 2 weeks, covered, and refrigerated. Reheat over a low flame.

CHOCOLATE SYRUP

Makes about 3 cups

This is a simple chocolate syrup that can be a sauce, stirred into milk to make chocolate milk, or swirled through the ice cream of your choice. When ready to use, bring to room temperature or heat over a low flame.

EQUIPMENT: medium saucepan, whisk, fine-mesh strainer, medium heatproof bowl

2 CUPS GRANULATED SUGAR

1 CUP UNSWEETENED COCOA POWDER

1 CUP BOILING WATER

1 TEASPOON VANILLA EXTRACT

In a medium saucepan, whisk together the sugar, cocoa, and boiling water. Over medium heat, bring just to a boil (bubbles forming around the edges of the syrup), whisking continuously, about 10 minutes. Boil 3 to 5 minutes, lower the heat, and simmer 3 minutes longer, stirring occasionally. Remove from the heat and stir in the vanilla. Pour through a fine-mesh strainer into a medium heatproof bowl. When cool, the syrup can be refrigerated and used as needed. The syrup thickens as it chills.

TO PREPARE AHEAD: The syrup will keep refrigerated, covered, for up to 2 weeks.

CHOCOLATE CURLS

Chocolate Curls make an ordinary dessert look spectacular, but keep in mind that they do take practice! Below are two methods used in many pastry kitchens, the first one perhaps more practical for the home kitchen. You can decide which you feel more comfortable doing.

Chocolate Curls can be made with any kind of chocolate—white, milk, or bittersweet. A thin-blade putty knife can be purchased in a hardware store, a pallet knife in an art supply store.

EQUIPMENT: medium heatproof bowl, flat baking tray, offset spatula, pallet knife, putty knife, or vegetable peeler

FIRST METHOD: In a medium heatproof bowl set over a pan of simmering water, melt 8 ounces of chocolate that has been broken into pieces. Heat a flat baking tray over a low flame for 30 seconds. Carefully remove from the heat, and invert on a flat surface. Pour the melted chocolate over the back of the tray and spread with an offset spatula, giving you a thin layer of chocolate. Refrigerate until set.

Remove from the refrigerator and let rest 5 or 10 minutes. Using a pallet knife or putty knife, make curls by pushing down and sliding the knife forward into the chocolate.

SECOND METHOD: This has to be done with a large block (at least 1 pound) of chocolate. Carefully wave the chocolate back and forth over a high flame on the stove until it gets shiny, without melting. Place the block on a flat surface and scrape curls with a vegetable peeler. However, if you live in a warm climate and it's the middle of the summer, you probably can eliminate waving it over the flame.

CHOCOLATE BAND

A chocolate band wrapped around any simple cake makes a dramatic presentation. The band should be made when the cake is finished so that it can be wrapped before the chocolate hardens completely.

EQUIPMENT: ruler or tape measure, 1 sheet wax paper, about 20 inches long, long sharp knife or scissors, medium heatproof bowl, offset spatula, wide spatula

6 OUNCES BITTERSWEET CHOCOLATE, CUT INTO SMALL PIECES

1. Make the wax-paper band: Measure the height of the cake with a ruler and mark it across the length of a wax-paper strip long enough to wrap around the cake plus a little extra. Fold over the paper as marked, across the entire length of the paper. Cut along the fold with a long, sharp knife or a pair of scissors. Set the strip aside. It will be used to wrap around the cake.

2. Place the chocolate in a medium heatproof bowl set over a pan of simmering water. Do not let the bottom of the bowl touch the water or the chocolate may burn. When the chocolate is almost completely melted, remove from the heat and let continue to melt, stirring occasionally.

3. Lay the prepared length of wax paper on a flat surface in front of you. Scrape the chocolate out of the bowl onto the wax paper. With an offset spatula, spread the chocolate, as evenly as possible, over the entire surface of the paper, using long, even strokes. Some of the chocolate will spread onto the work surface, but that's okay. This can be cleaned up later. Immediately pick up each end of the wax paper band and transfer to a clean, smooth surface, keeping the band as straight as possible, and leaving enough room to place the cake directly in front of the band.

4. Wrap the band around the cake: Remove the cake from the refrigerator and set it directly in front of the center of the band. Pick up each end of the band and carefully wrap it around the cake, pinching the ends together and cutting off the excess "tail" with a pair of sharp scissors (see first two illustrations on opposite page). Refrigerate the cake, picking it up with a wide spatula. Do not touch the sides of the cake, since the chocolate band is still soft.

5. After 30 minutes, or when ready to serve, as with the ice cream cake, the cake can be removed from the refrigerator and the wax paper removed by gently peeling it from one end of the band to the other (see illustration). The cake can now be refrigerated until needed.

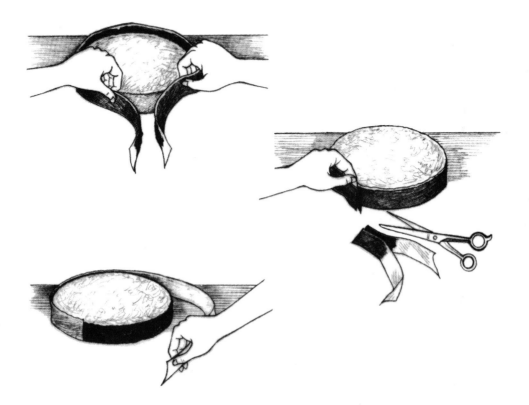

FRUIT COMPOTES

Here are three fruit compotes that can be used interchangeably, according to the season or to taste. It is always best to select fruit when it is at its ripest and full of flavor. The procedure applies to all three compotes, each one making about 2 cups.

EQUIPMENT: medium heavy nonreactive saucepan, long-handled wooden spoon

Strawberry Compote

3 PINTS STRAWBERRIES, CUT INTO THICK SLICES
¼ CUP GRANULATED SUGAR
1 VANILLA BEAN, SPLIT LENGTHWISE AND SCRAPED

Blackberry Compote

4 PINTS BLACKBERRIES
¼ CUP GRANULATED SUGAR
ZEST OF 1 MEDIUM LEMON, FINELY CHOPPED

Raspberry Compote

4 PINTS RASPBERRIES
¼ CUP GRANULATED SUGAR
ZEST OF 1 MEDIUM LEMON, FINELY CHOPPED

1. In a medium heavy nonreactive saucepan, combine the ingredients for each compote and cook over medium heat until the fruit exudes the juices. Turn the heat to low and cook until the compote thickens, about 15 minutes longer, stirring occasionally with a wooden spoon to make certain that the fruit does not stick to the bottom of the pan.

2. Remove from the heat and let cool. (If you are making Strawberry Compote, remove the vanilla bean.) Use as needed.

TO PREPARE AHEAD: Through step 2, the compote can be made ahead and refrigerated in an airtight container for 1 week.

SUGAR SYRUP

This simple syrup is a staple in all pastry kitchens, used to poach fruit, make sorbets, and moisten cakes. It can also be used to sweeten iced drinks.

EQUIPMENT: large saucepan

3 CUPS WATER

2⅓ CUPS GRANULATED SUGAR

In a large saucepan, combine the water and sugar, and stir to mix well. Over medium heat, bring to a boil and continue to boil until the mixture is clear and the sugar is completely dissolved, 3 to 5 minutes. Cool. When cool, pour into a jar, cover, and refrigerate. Use as needed.

TO PREPARE AHEAD: The Sugar Syrup will keep tightly covered in the refrigerator almost indefinitely.

INGREDIENTS AND SUGGESTED EQUIPMENT

• • •

INGREDIENTS

BAKING POWDER AND BAKING SODA: These are added to flour to lighten the mixture by distributing CO_2 during the baking process, causing the batter to rise. They cannot be used interchangeably. Baking soda (also known as sodium bicarbonate), an alkali, must combine with an acid—such as buttermilk or sour milk—to release the gas. Baking powder consists of baking soda and cream of tartar, an acid. The chemical reaction takes place when any liquid is added.

BUTTER: Unsalted butter is used throughout this book. Choose Grade AA butter if possible. Do not use whipped butter; because air is whipped into it, it is not solid butter.

COCOA POWDER: Cocoa powder is available in most markets. Dutch-process cocoa powder, which is what we have used in our recipes, is rich, dark in color, and mild-flavored. The cocoa powder is unsweetened.

CREAM: When recipes call for heavy cream, it is cream that can be whipped. Heavy cream should contain at least 40 percent butterfat for best results when whipping. Chill the bowl and beaters first, then pour the cream into the bowl. Start slowly so that the cream does not splatter, and increase the speed as the cream thickens.

EGGS: All of the recipes in the book are based on eggs graded "large," unless otherwise specified. When adding eggs, break one egg at a time into a small cup and then add it to the batter. It is best to separate eggs when they are cold, and then allow the eggs to come to room temperature. The egg whites must go into a perfectly clean bowl, free of water, grease, or any trace of yolk, to maximize the volume. The bowl can be copper, stainless steel, or glass. If the yolk goes into the whites, remove it by dipping an eggshell half into the whites and letting the yolk particles float into it.

FLOURS: *All-purpose flour* is a blend of high-gluten hard and low-gluten soft wheat flours. The flours come bleached or unbleached, and either kind can be used. *Cake flour* is made from soft wheat flour, and we use it in combination with all-purpose flour for a flakier puff pastry. *Pastry flour* is softer than all-purpose flour but not as soft as cake flour and can be purchased in specialty food shops.

To measure flour, scoop enough flour into a dry measuring cup to slightly overflow the cup. (You should use the exact size cup needed.) Remove the excess flour by scraping the back of a knife or straight metal spatula across the top of the cup. Flour can be sifted onto wax or parchment paper or into a bowl.

OILS: When a recipe calls for vegetable oil, it can be safflower, corn, or canola.

SALT: Kosher salt is used in all of our recipes (unless otherwise specified). It melts easily into the batters and has a lighter taste than iodized salt.

SUGAR: *Granulated sugar* is extracted from sugarcane and beets. It is the most familiar and most commonly used of the sugars. A simple carbohydrate, it is nearly pure sucrose. It can be ground to a finer consistency in a blender or food processor. *Brown sugar* is a mixture of white sugar and molasses, light brown having less molasses than the dark brown. When measuring, you should firmly pack it down. Brown sugar tends to harden as it stands and should be stored in a tightly closed container in a cool spot. *Confectioners' sugar,* also called powdered sugar or 10× sugar, is sugar ground to a fine powdery texture and mixed with a small amount of starch to prevent caking. It always should be sifted before measuring. *Crystal sugar* consists of large, clear crystals, larger than granulated sugar. It usually can be purchased in specialty food shops.

VANILLA BEAN: The vanilla bean has a flavor that cannot be duplicated. To impart the taste, the bean is split down the center and the seeds scraped out. To store the bean, wrap it securely and refrigerate. In most of our recipes, pure vanilla extract is used, because vanilla beans are quite expensive.

SUGGESTED EQUIPMENT

BAKING DISH: At least one $8\frac{1}{2} \times 11$-inch dish.

BAKING PANS: Two $12 \times 17 \times 1$-inch pans. Since we recommend lining pans with parchment paper, a coated pan is not necessary. A heavy-duty stainless steel pan will last longer than aluminum and will not warp when baking at high temperatures.

BAKING TRAYS (COOKIE SHEETS): We suggest at least two cookie sheets so that one can be cooling while the other is being used. (See above for use of stainless steel for baking pans.)

BOWLS, MIXING: Small, medium, and large bowls, preferably stainless steel. Stainless steel can be used for melting or whisking ingredients over hot water as well as for mixing ingredients that are chilled or at room temperature. However, any *heatproof* bowl can be used.

CAKE PANS: Two 8- or 9-inch round pans.

CAKE RACK: Two 11×17-inch racks. This size is most useful because it will hold many cookies and different-sized cakes.

CANDY THERMOMETER

CARDBOARD CAKE ROUNDS: Can be purchased at cookware supply shops. The rounds are slipped under cakes before decorating or placing on a service plate.

COOKIE CUTTERS: You can substitute whatever you have that approximates the size suggested for the particular recipe.

COOKIE SHEETS: *See* Baking trays.

ELECTRIC MIXER: The Kitchen Aid comes with paddle, whip, and dough hook. Others come with beaters and dough hook. We specify which attachment is to be used in each recipe.

FOOD PROCESSOR: Used to make purees and some of the pastries.

LADLES: 2- and 4-ounce capacity.

MEASURING CUPS: It is a good idea to have two sets for dry ingredients. The cups come in graduated sizes, from ¼ to 1 cup. They should have smooth, flat rims to facilitate leveling the ingredients; to level, run a knife or spatula across the top of the cup. You should also have 2-cup and 4-cup measuring cups for liquids. These cups have spouts on one end for easier pouring. They come in Pyrex or heavy-duty plastic.

MEASURING SPOONS: These usually come in sets, with ¼, ½, and 1 teaspoon and one tablespoon. For convenience, have two sets.

OVEN MITTS

OVEN THERMOMETER

PARCHMENT PAPER: Used for lining cake pans, this is now available precut in various sizes to fit round or square pans. It also comes in rolls.

PASTRY BAGS WITH VARIOUS-SIZED TIPS: The bags should be cloth, soft nylon, or heavy-duty plastic, 10 or 12 inches long.

PASTRY BRUSHES: One small and one large. The brushes should have soft natural bristles. Do not use brushes with plastic bristles, since these tend to burn or melt. Brand-new paintbrushes are perfect. Brushes can be washed in the dishwasher.

PIE PLATES: 9- and/or 10-inch plates, preferably Pyrex.

PIE WEIGHTS: These are tiny metal, ceramic, or plastic weights that can be purchased at cookware or specialty food shops. They are used when prebaking pie shells to prevent the shells from shrinking. Dried beans are just as effective. Weights and beans can be reused; cool, remove from pie shells, and store.

PIPING BAG: A cone-shaped bag made out of parchment paper (see illustrations at top of next page).

PROPANE TORCH: Optional, but useful for many recipes. Directions must be carefully followed. Torches can be purchased in hardware and/or building supply stores. Williams-Sonoma also sells a mini-torch that uses butane rather than propane.

ROLLING PIN: We prefer a French rolling pin without handles, but it is important to be comfortable with whatever you do use.

RULER: Keep a 12-inch ruler exclusively for kitchen use.

SAUCEPANS: 1-quart and 2-quart heavy, nonreactive saucepans.

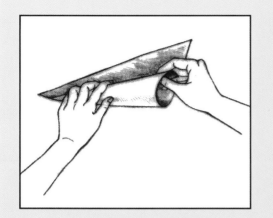
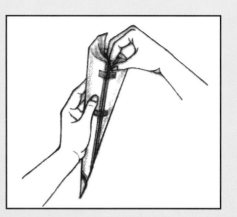

HOW TO MAKE A PIPING BAG:
CUT PARCHMENT PAPER INTO THE SHAPE OF A TRIANGLE. WRAP IT TIGHTLY TO CREATE A CONE WITH A VERY SMALL OPENING AT THE TIP (SEE PHOTO LEFT). TAPE CLOSED (SEE PHOTO RIGHT). THIS TAKES PRACTICE!

SCALE: A scale that holds 3 pounds of ingredients should be adequate. It may be practical to purchase a scale that registers grams as well as pounds, since some cookbooks list recipes in grams.

SIFTER: A large fine-mesh strainer with a wooden handle is just as serviceable as a sifter. It can be used to sift your dry ingredients as well as to strain ice cream bases, compotes, etc.

SLIPAT SHEETS: These can be used in place of parchment paper, transforming an ordinary baking sheet into a nonstick one. They can be found in cookware supply shops.

SOUFFLÉ DISHES: Six ¾-cup ovenproof dishes.

SPATULAS: 1 wide metal spatula; 1 long, thin metal spatula; 2 large and 2 small rubber spatulas; and 1 offset spatula.

SPRINGFORM PANS: 8- and 9-inch pans.

SQUEEZE BOTTLE: A plastic bottle with a twist-off top that has a tiny opening on the end. We fill the bottle with a sauce and then squeeze the sauce through the opening, decorating dessert plates just before they are taken to the table.

STRAINER: *See* Sifter.

TART PANS WITH REMOVABLE BOTTOMS: 9- and/or 10-inch pans made of heavy-duty aluminum or stainless steel.

TIMER

TOWELS: Keep kitchen towels on hand when baking. Dry, they are more useful than pot holders, and wet, they can be used for cleanups. *Never* use a wet towel to handle a hot pot or pan. Heat is conducted through a wet towel and can burn your hand.

WHISKS: 2 balloon whisks, 12 to 16 inches long (including the handle). When you don't want to or can't use an electric mixer, these are very convenient for whipping eggs or cream. The thinner and more flexible the wire, the better the whisk.

WOODEN SPOONS: 2 long-handled and 2 short-handled.

ZESTER

TEMPERING CHOCOLATE

. . .

*T*empering chocolate is a process of regulating the cocoa butter to prevent discoloration and streaking. If you are melting chocolate for cake or frosting, you don't have to temper it, but it should be tempered when it will be used for molding or as a sauce for dipping.

Chocolate is tempered to slow the streaking (or "bloom," as it is sometimes called) that can appear on its outer surface. Untempered chocolate can look dull. Tempering reestablishes its glossiness.

A simple way to accomplish this is to finely chop the amount of chocolate needed and place three-quarters of it in the top of a double boiler, reserving one quarter to add when the chocolate is cooled. Do not cover the chocolate because condensation will form, and water and chocolate do not mix. And don't let the water in the bottom pan touch the pan with the chocolate. Melt the chocolate over simmering—not bubbling—water. Using a candy thermometer, bring the chocolate to 115 to 120 degrees Fahrenheit. Remove the chocolate from the heat and add the reserved chocolate, stirring to combine thoroughly and to cool. Dark chocolate should be cooled to 88 to 90 degrees, milk and white chocolate to 84 to 88 degrees.

The chocolate can now be used for dipping or molding. Leftover chocolate can be hardened, broken into pieces, wrapped in foil, and stored in a cool spot for future use.

HOW TO PREPARE AND
FROST A LAYER CAKE

. . .

*T*o cut a cake into layers, place the cake on a flat, firm work surface, rounded side up. Using a long, serrated knife, starting at the outer edge of the cake, carefully trim away just the rounded dome of the cake, leaving a flat top.

Using a ruler, measure the height of the cake and then divide by 2 or 3 or however many layers you want. (If the cake is 3 inches high and you want two layers, each layer would be 1½ inches thick; for three layers it would be 1 inch thick.)

Insert toothpicks like spokes, 1 inch apart, into the side of the cake around the diameter at the exact point at which you want to slice the cake. Place one hand on top of the cake and gradually slice the cake horizontally, just above the circle of toothpicks but not completely through the cake, turning the cake as you slice. After you have made a complete circle with the knife, carefully slide the knife from one side of the cake to the other. You have just cut the cake into two layers. Set the layers aside. Repeat this process with the ruler and toothpicks if you are making more than one layer.

Arrange the layers on a flat surface and brush away any excess crumbs with a soft pastry brush. Save the most level layer for the top of the cake.

Place the first cake layer on a cardboard round slightly larger than the cake. With a small offset spatula, cover the first layer with a thin layer of frosting. Set the second cake layer on top, gently pressing down to secure. If there are more layers, cover as above. Using a long metal spatula, remove any excess frosting from the sides of the cake. Chill until the frosting sets, about 30 minutes in the refrigerator or 10 minutes in the freezer.

When ready, brush away any excess crumbs from the top and place all but 1 cup of frosting on the cake. Spread with the small offset spatula, covering the top and sides of the cake. With a clean long spatula, level the frosting, making it as smooth as possible. Spoon the remaining cup of frosting into a small pastry bag fitted with a #1 star tip. Pipe a latticework pattern on top of the cake and a border all around its base.

Refrigerate until firm, at least 30 minutes. Run the blade of a long knife under the cake, then slip a wide spatula under the cake and transfer to a clean plate. Refrigerate until needed, removing about 30 minutes before serving.

EQUIPMENT: long serrated knife, ruler, toothpicks, cardboard round, small offset spatula, long metal spatula, pastry bag with #1 star tip, wide metal spatula

TO PREPARE AHEAD: The cake can be made and finished 1 day ahead of serving.

ACKNOWLEDGMENTS

. . .

There are many people we would like to thank for their help with this project: Tom Kaplan, David Robins, the entire pastry department of Spago Las Vegas, Chris Humphrey, Dave Meadows, Chelle Meldram, Madeline Benito, and Barbara Beckenstein.

We would also like to thank our agent, Janis Donnaud, as well as Joy de Menil, Beth Pearson, Robbin Schiff, Barbara Bachman, and Susan Di Sesa of Random House.

It was a delight working with Alan Richardson, our talented photographer. And many thanks to John DeSourdie and Zinna and Lois Mathias for helping us with the desserts that were photographed.

We are especially grateful to Wolfgang Puck and Barbara Lazaroff. Without their encouragement, this book would not have happened.

INDEX

. . .

ABOUT THE AUTHORS

MARY BERGIN is one of the longest-standing veterans of Spago, where she has worked since the first Spago restaurant was founded in the early eighties. She was head pastry chef at Spago Los Angeles from 1987 to 1992, when she moved to Spago Las Vegas. She contributed recipes to Wolfgang Puck's *Adventures in the Kitchen* and is the co-author of *Spago Desserts*. One of the stars of Julia Child's *Cooking with Master Chefs*, she has appeared on the Food Network, *Good Morning America*, and *The Home Show*. She encourages her two children, Jackie and Anthony, to play an active role in tasting and experimenting in the kitchen.

JUDY GETHERS, whose family has owned Ratner's, a landmark New York City restaurant, since 1905, grew up in and around kitchens. She is the author of *The World Famous Ratner's Meatless Cookbook, Italian Country Cooking,* and (with Mary Bergin) *Spago Desserts*. She collaborated with Wolfgang Puck on *The Wolfgang Puck Cookbook* and *Adventures in the Kitchen.*

ABOUT THE PHOTOGRAPHER

ALAN RICHARDSON is an award-winning photographer whose work has been featured in *Condé Nast Traveler, Esquire, Food & Wine, GQ, Self, Vogue, The New York Times Magazine,* and *The Washington Post Magazine.* He was the photographer for *The Four Seasons of Italian Cooking.*